ALPHA AND OMEGA

by

DAVID JONES

4th July, 2009.

To my dearest friends

nearly - next - door,

Thankyou for your very welcome

and vivifying T.L.C.

In the Lord,

Fr. David

ORIGINAL WRITING

ISBN: 978-1-906018-98-6

A CIP catalogue for this book is available from the National Library.

Published by Original Writing Ltd., Dublin, 2009.

Printed in Ireland by Cahill Printers Limited.

FOREWORD

The contents of the present volume represents the poetic journal of a Welsh monk who was formed for many years in the Carthusian life in France but largely because of his poetic activity was obliged to transfer to another monastery, where that particular aspect of life was felt to be less incongruous. Except for the periods in which in France the activity was not encouraged, the journal has been maintained since 1980.

Much of the earlier work was analysed in detail by Dr Eva Schmid-Mörwald, in a brilliant doctoral thesis, subsequently published in the *Analecta Cartusiana* in 1994, under the title of *The Lyre and the Cross*.

The author's one desire from school days was immediate entry into a monastic novitiate, in a strictly contemplative house. Monastic life in French houses being often of an intense and powerful brand, he opted for the Carthusian life in a small house, now closed, unfortunately, as it was an excellent monastery. However, a certain opposition on the part of the Mother-house made it difficult to combine the monastic life with that of poetic and musical composition.

His Irish spiritual father eventually advised him to enter an Irish monastery, and although he was later transferred to a new foundation in Italy, where he was able to be of use as guest master and then also novice master, he was given permission to return to Ireland, where, thanks to the kind support of the Bishop of Meath, he is now living a quiet eremitic life in front of the ruins of St Kienan's monastery in Duleek, a name which would suggest that it was originally a very early stone-built church.

The Celtic bond of affinity which binds the Welsh to the Irish may be seen in the occasional use of Welsh and frequent references to the Irish character and way of life in this volume, which covers the dramatic period in which the long desired return to the purely eremitic state, in a Celtic context, was actually made to happen, not without insistence. As one Abbot President once discreetly put it, the operative principle is: "Get behind the Abbot, and push."

In the present volume, which covers the period 2000-2009, the sweat involved in such pushing emerges. The period here covered is one in which many upheavals took place. That explains why the early part of the work is situated in an Italian and French context (French being often the language of day to day life in the monastery), while the final part is situated in a more Celtic (Irish-Welsh) atmosphere.

Thanks to the kindness of clergy and friends, the writer is now living quietly in a hermitage in an area already hallowed by prayer from the earliest times. It is therefore an ancient flame that burns again in the unchanged Celtic night.

Ausculta. Ausculta, fili mi,
Verborum conchas aperi,
Ne in his se abscondat Veritas
Et Transeuntem transeas.

Va lentement, va lentement,
Respire, aspire doucement
La grâce d'une vérité
Échappée de l'éternité.

Whoe'er thou be that readest this,
Tread slowly, softly – for the kiss,
The sense, the inward sense, the bliss
Of passing Truth much haste did miss.

Clyw, aros, clyw, ac aros eto awr
Gyfoethog yn ei hedd, a'r bedd a ddaw
Heb ruthr am a ddaeth, cans yma iaith
Adweinir lle cyffyrddwyd rhyw hoff baith.

Introduction

Born in Cardiff on 16 November 1953 to Welsh parents with considerable cultural interests, the author was brought up in an ambience where religious practice played a considerable role in daily life. In 1967, in the lead-up to a Billy Graham summer campaign, he experienced an inner "conversion" and was baptised in the Baptist Chapel at Cardiff on 8 October 1967, assuming full membership of that community on 15 October. His indefatigable quest to know God was, however, only beginning. Soon his reading convinced him that the truth in all its fulness lay with the Roman Catholic Church, but, owing to his youth, his parents and mentors advised him to wait awhile before seeking admission, though he already tended to attend mass rather than the services in the local Baptist chapel. On Holy Saturday, 10 April 1971, he was, however, "reconciled" to the Catholic Church by Dom Edmund Hatton (novice master), on behalf of his spiritual director, Dom Laurence Bénevot, in St. David's chapel in the crypt of Ampleforth Abbey.

After taking his A levels in the summer of 1972, he stayed on at school till Easter 1973, so that he might learn Greek. With impulsive generosity he immediately wished to enter Prinknash Abbey near Gloucester, a community of Benedictines of the Primitive Observance, who enjoyed a reputation for austerity. However, in view of his recent conversion and the fact that he had been awarded a scholarship for university studies, he was advised to take his degree first and went off to study Latin, Greek and Philosophy at the University College of Wales in Aberystwyth, where he graduated with joint honours in Latin and Greek in 1976. His monastic journey then began in earnest. After a stay at La Grande Trappe in Normandy, he made a retreat at the charterhouse of Sélignac near Bourg-en-Bresse before entering the Carthusian Order on 20 December 1976. It was at Sélignac that Dom David, as he was called in religion, began after a time to write poetry seriously, taking for his material his inner experiences in his search for the divine. If some echoes of Wordsworth, Coleridge and Hopkins are apparent, the monk at once found his own voice, and the reader is left in no doubt as regards the immediacy of the experiences depicted in *The Threshold of Paradise*.[1]. Eva Schmid-Mörwald, writing in the preface to Paradise Regained[2], reveals her reaction to this first volume:

When I first came across The Threshold of Paradise, *a collection of verse written by a contemporary Welsh novice monk, I was stirred by the enthralling spirit radiating from the poems. The novice's love and reverence for the Creator were startling. Here a man was celebrating his love for God by creating poems of subtle beauty. His happiness was not unblemished though, for*

1   Anon., *The Threshold of Paradise: The Poetic Journal of a Welsh Novice Monk* , in *Analecta Cartusiana* 129 (1988), v-xii, 1-90. The volume was republished with a preface by the present writer and a blurb by Eva Schmid Mörwald as: A Monk, *The Threshold of Paradise*, Adelphi Press, London 1994. Some of the poems were also reprinted in A Welsh Novice Monk, *Poems Sacred and Profane, Salzburg Studies in English Literature, Poetic Drama & Poetic Theory* 68:3 (1988), 5-45.
2   Anon. [A Welsh Novice Monk], *Paradise Regained, Salzburg Studies in English Literature, Poetic Drama & Poetic Theory* 146 (1996), iii.

the road to perfection is a long and stony path, as was reflected in the verse. These poems grippingly captured the circumstances of their origin and whilst reading them I was bound to grasp some of the enormous inner tension that must have been present at their origin. I could feel the poet's urge to express his feelings and find an outlet for them. My interest was aroused: poet AND monk? The lines I had been reading were no feeble attemps in versifying, for they had a voice of their own; however, the two concepts of being both a monk true to heaven and a poet true to earth seemed to be too different to blend, particularly as it was the work of a Carthusian monk I had been reading. Wasn't that a contradiction in itself? Could these two vocations really be successfully united, sustaining each other in perfect symbiosis without doing harm to one [an]other?

Brother David's monastic vocation is highly interwoven with his poetic vocation; there is a strong original link between his call to solitude and his urge to write poetry. For him the writing of poetry represents a means to praise his Creator but also serves as an outlet for accumulated feelings. The poet's urge to write is nurtured by his boundless belief in and love for God, the poems stem from the intensity of his religious experience. His first poetic volumes adopt the form of a diary, where we find poems as diary entries. They reflect the spiritual journey of their author in all its intensity and invite the reader to partake. Periods of unbound happiness and joy, when feeling the closeness to God, as well as times of appalling grief, disappointment and loneliness, when experiencing His absence, are captured in his verse, their honest straightforwardness leaving the reader dazed at times.[3]

3 In her blurb for Anon., *Ad Maiestatem: The Journal of a Welsh Monk*,

The Threshold of Paradise indeed mirrors the devotion of a Carthusian monk and his inner struggles, offering glimpses of an austerity unequalled by any other Catholic Order. Unfortunately, the authorities of the Order felt — rightly or wrongly — that Dom David did not possess a purely Carthusian vocation, and, after his seven years of probation, he was not admitted to solemn vows, leaving the Order on 25 March 1984 on the expiration of his temporary vows.4

After a period of reflection, including retreats at Quarr Abbey and St. Hugh's Charterhouse near Horsham, Dom David decided to enter La Grande Trappe, a monastery that had always fascinated him. His volume A World within the World: The Poetic Journal of a Welsh Novice Monk5 reflects his experiences as a Cistercian

Salzburg Studies in English Literature, Poetic Drama & Poetic Theory 146:2 (1997), she expresses similar sentiments: "His verse reflects the austere life in a Carthusian cell, mirroring a whole world which usually is firmly closed off from the rest of mankind outside the monastic walls. The firmness of his belief, assailed nevertheless by spiritual struggles, utmost despair as opposed to ecstatic happiness, the fruits of silence contrasted by desperate loneliness, represent an immensely fruitful source for his poetry ... his musings merge into a poetry not only of high spiritual value but also offer great æsthetic pleasure. The sonnet proves to be the poet's favourire verse form, a remarkable fact, as traditional verse forms, in particular such demanding ones as the sonnet, do not enjoy great popularity nowadays." Eva Schmid-Mörwald is also responsible for two major studies of Dom David's poetry: "Poetry in the Order: A Welsh Novice Monk", in James Hogg, Karl Hubmayer, & Dorothea Steiner (eds.), *English Language and Literature: Positions and Dispositions, Salzburger Studien zur Anglistik und Amerikanistik* 16 (1990), 73-82, and *The Lyre and the Cross in the Poetry of Alun Idris Jones, Analecta Cartusiana* 129:2 (1994), a study containing detailed analyses of the poems and furnishing an excellent bibliography.
4   Dom Augustin Devaux, *La Poésie Latine chez les Chartreux, Analecta Cartusiana* 131 (1997), reveals, however, that a fair number of Carthusians did indulge in writing poetry. He devotes pp. 426-29 to Dom David Jones.
5   *Salzburg Studies in English Literature, Poetic Drama & Poetic Theory* 68:2 (1988).

monk of the Strict Observance, but here again his aspirations were disappointed, despite the undoubted seriousness of his intentions, which are clearly revealed in such poems as "The twenty-fifth of March 1984".6 The sonnet became his preferred verse-form for depicting his spiritual journey on the stony road to perfection. The chapter of La Grande Trappe held the opinion that writing poetry was irreconcilable with the Cistercian vocation, so, after nearly two years of trial, he moved on to the Trappist abbey of Roscrea in Southern Ireland, hoping to find the monks there more sympathetic to his poetic bent. Unfortunately for him Roscrea is unusual in running a school, which inevitably diminishes the seclusion of the monks to a certain extent. He struggled on for a time, but eventually left and returned to Wales on 20 June 1986. Far from being disillusioned, he was full of plans, contemplating becoming a recluse or even trying to re-establish monastic life in North Wales. At other moments he thought of engaging in the Charismatic Renewal in France. As no concrete possibility offered itself, he resumed studies at the Normal College in Bangor on 8 September 1986, obtaining a graduate diploma in primary education the following year. The pull of the monastic life had by no means diminished, and he made retreats at a number of houses, before settling in for a prolonged stay at Ealing Abbey, a Benedictine house affiliated to the English Congregation in the suburbs of London. There he was advised to seek out a community more exclusively devoted to the contemplative life. Rather rashly, he chose Farnborough Abbey, not far from London, a house that had changed over from the Solesmes Congregation to that of Subiaco, but which somehow had never flourished. No doubt, he was attracted by the musical tradition of the monks. He began his official postulancy there on 7 March 1988 and was clothed

---

6 Printed in *The Threshold of Paradise, Analecta Cartusiana* edition, 90.

in the Benedictine habit on 10 December of that year, the Feast of St. John Roberts, taking the name of that Saint. The young novice did not find Farnborough as congenial as he had hoped. The community was small and passed through a dolorous crisis. Furthermore, the monks were heavily engaged in looking after the parish, which reduced the time available for a more strictly contemplative life. Early in 1989 he realized that he would not find fulfilment there and returned to Wales, where he resided at Talacre Abbey with Dom Basil Heath-Robinson, the former prior of Farnborough, for five weeks, pondering on the possibility of initiating a Benedictine foundation in North Wales. Though the Abbot of Ramsgate, Dom Gilbert Jones, was favourable to the venture, the local bishop was unsympathetic and withheld his approval. From April onwards the poet was enlisted on a project for translating the Church Fathers into Modern English.7 At the start of the new academic year, in the autumn of 1989, the poet enlisted for the Bachelor of Divinity course at University College, Bangor. Owing to his previous studies he was allowed to condense the three years into two, graduating in June 1991. Meanwhile he had been reflecting on the future. His spiritual director, Dr. John Ryan, O.M.I., felt that the Premonstratensian Order, with its ordered liturgy and tradition of study and prayer in community, might be the long sought-for haven. He established contacts with Holy Trinity Abbey at Kilnacrott in County Cavan, Ireland. The poet entered this community on the Feast of St. Luke, 18 October 1991, and took the habit on the Feast of the Immaculate Conception, celebrated on 9 December that year. He reverted to the religious name Dom David. After the first year of his novitiate he recommenced theological studies in Dublin. The

---

7 This resulted in Oliver Davies, *Promise of Good Things. The Apostolic Fathers*. Translations by Alun Idris Jones and Oliver Davies, London 1992.

volume A World beyond the World[8] depicts his experiences at Farnborough, his time as a student at Bangor, and his novitiate at Kilnacrott. Inevitably, student life reveals different atmospherics to the daily round of the cloister, but his unalloyed joy at re-entering the religious life, where he might devote himself to God alone, is unmistakable. On 8 December 1993 he made his profession as a Premonstratensian. A few weeks later, on 30 January 1994, he was sent to study Spritual Theology at the Angelicum in Rome, residing at the Premonstratensian house in the eternal city. He had learnt enough Italian in Dublin to get by, and as the canons at Kilnacrott engaged in pastoral and youth work, it was felt that such a course of study would be helpful to him in counselling work later. At last, all seemed to have settled to a calm, which is reflected in his poems of the time, but further tempests were brewing up. Kilnacrott hit the headlines in the national press as a result of an unfortunate scandal. The superior was changed and even the future of the abbey seemed in jeopardy. He was able to present his minor thesis in the early summer of 1995,[9] but was then ordered to return to Ireland. He obeyed, leaving Rome on 18 June, but, owing to the turmoil at the abbey, he requested six months' leave of absence to reflect upon the situation. This was granted and Dom David resided for a time at Mount Tabor Hermitage in the west of Ireland, which had recently been consecrated by the Archbishop of Tuam. The solution could only be temporary, as he was not yet in Holy Orders, and therefore could not really act as chaplain. That summer my wife and I had by chance visited the magnificent romanesque abbey of Sant'Antimo,

---

8 *Analecta Cartusiana* 129:3 (1993).
9 This has been printed as Br. David Jones, "Adam Scot: The tension in the psyche of the man of prayer between active and contemplative life", in *The Mystical Tradition and the Carthusians, Analecta Cartusiana* 130:11 (1996), 1-37.

in a remote corner of Tuscany, where a small community, mainly from France, follow the Premonstratensian rule and sing the whole of the Office to the original Gregorian melodies in Latin in the abbey church. We were duly impressed, and, knowing of the crisis at Kilnacrott, we suggested to Dom David that this might be something for him. He duly arrived at the Abbazia near Castelnuovo dell'Abate on 6 December 1995, and though he hesitated to leave the official Premonstratensian Order for some weeks, as several poems in the present volume reveal,10 he finally decided to join the community at Sant'Antimo, where he made his solemn profession on 9 December 1996, and was ordained to the priesthood in Siena's beautiful medieval cathedral on 31 October 1997. Soon thereafter he returned to the Angelicum, where he presented a doctoral thesis of the highest distinction in December 1998.11 He now occupies the combined posts of sacristan and guest-master at Sant'Antimo, and since March 2000 has also been given charge of the novitiate.

Some poems from this period were printed in *Ad Maiestatem*,12 but this new collection gives a much more detailed overall picture of the poet's spiritual pilgrimage from the time of his first studies in Rome up to the present. A much greater tranquillity is immediately apparent, even if some longings remain unsatisfied.

As in previous volumes, the poet shows himself to be an expert linguist, writing with equal facility in Welsh, English, French, Italian, Latin and Greek. There are no poems as yet in German, though there are several German headings, and after residences

---

10 Cf. particularly the poem "Rome".
11 Printed as Br. David Jones, *An Early Witness to the Nature of the Canonical Order in the Twelfth Century: A Study in the Life and Writings of Adam Scot, with Particular Reference to his Understanding of the Rule of St. Augustine, Analecta Cartusiana* 151 (1999).
12 Several poems are reprinted in the present volume.

at Wilten Abbey near Innsbruck and with the Benedictines in Augsburg to learn the language, it only seems a matter of time before he tries his hand in that language too.

Dom David is not an avant-garde poet. In some respects the poems in the slim volume recently issued for a monk of Parkminster are more "modern" in their texture, but the slightly archaic tone on occasion has been deliberately chosen as appropriate to clothe the religious content. The topics are almost exclusively concerned with the daily round of the religious life, and we see the poet learning to say the mass, listen to his innermost thoughts about his profession and ordination, his joy in celebrating the mass in abbeys and churches that had meant much to him in the past, his administering the sacraments and preaching retreats, even as far away as at a nunnery in Rumania, his enthusiasm for pilgrimages, such as Medugorje, which the present writer has always felt rather reserved about, as also for Dom David's enthusiasm for miracles, wonders and signs.[13]   Even after his ordination, he was still dreaming of restoring the monastic life in Wales, as "Penmon" reveals, and his fascination with the solitary life as led by the Carthusian and Camaldolese Orders remained, as we see in "This is the day", "A New Reverend Father", "Chartreuse", "Letter from the Grande Chartreuse", "Unopened", "Eve of Saint Romuald", "Recluso", "Eremo", "Dom Damien",[14] "Reading lines penned beside Dom Damien's tomb", "Haunted", and "Letter to a friend".

It may be significant that, despite its French title,[15] he chose to write his profession poem in Welsh. However, there are poems in

13   This enthusiasm was apparent in earlier volumes of verse and in Alun Idris Jones, *The Purgatory Manuscript. Le Manuscrit du Purgatoire*, Studies in Women and Religion 29, Lewiston, N.Y. 1990.
14   Dom Damien had been a Carthusian at Sélignac, but he transferred to Camaldoli and died as a recluse there.
15   "Vous ferez la profession le neuf décembre", reflecting the Prior's own words.

English revealing the depths of his feelings about his profession and ordination, which cannot fail to move the reader:

Vous avez été accepté
(à l'unanimité)

O! joy on earth! O! joy yet in the world!
To know that I am Thine, and Thine shall be,
And Thine alone, and by a little word
Upon this altar placed, eternally
To this Thy temple joined ó to know that now
No man or angel fiend can mar the road
Trod here by friends now crowned, that once did bow
Here where I place my head: to see the cloud
Of witnesses unseen walk calmly by
And chuckle at an æon, to see all
Melt in a moment felt, nay, and to cry
A tear of blissful peace ó this is to call
From out of the abyss of Failure vast,
And clutch at but a notch of grace at last.

or:
In petram inaccessam mihi deduc me

O joy! I shall yet hold Thee in my hand
Upon this ancient stone where others felt
The passing of their God: I shall there stand
Where souls have stood before and angels knelt
At veilèd Mystery ó I see the light

Of Tabor in this night, for this one word
Of manhood made is weighed with Godhead's might,
And in one chrismic sound I have all heard.
O Master of this astral path we tread,
I hear, I hear the voice that never was
By mortals caught, and here my little head
I bow to Thy great blessing: this day has
A ray of touch electric hither sent,
And o'er a sound the heavy cosmos bent.

or:

How beautiful are the feet of those who bear good tidings
[Prior's news of Dom David's ordination]
"C'est un des jours les plus heureux de ma vie!"

O! bliss in but a sound! O! happy day,
That changes every day for evermore,
That brings back yesterday from far away,
And sparkles with a grace once known before!
A word this hour was heard that has a pow'r
Beyond the noise of scribblings and of hands
Not driven from above; nay, one small hour
O'er years of heavy waiting calmly stands.
My God, I shall Thee touch, I shall Thee hold,
And be Thy voice on earth ó I shall be free
To climb these ancient steps and there be bold
To walk alone 'mid clouded Trinity.
I shall, hid Friend, for ever and a day,
A Priest be, till the æons fade away.

Less exclusively autobiographical, and therefore applicable to us all in these days of super-activism, is:

What is this life?

("J'ai gaspillé ma vie à faire trop de choses ...")

(Paroles d'un Chartreux)

There is too much to do on earth, and more
Than need be done is done by all that do
Too much to do all well, for this one law
Of patient moments old, that ancients knew,
The new-found sound of man can ill contain,
And waning is the moon that should have known
To slowly be, to wholly be again
What once it calmly was to days outblown.
O Master of the energies of flesh,
That twitch and chatter o'er a loudest day
That held a bulging load, what did enmesh
The very brain that breathed, till it should pay
A debt too heavy to a great machine
That had no pow'r to stop till all had been?

The present volume not only offers a graphic portrayal of the pilgrimage of a soul willingly and unreservedly placed in God's hands in often arrestingly beautiful poetic diction, but also exudes much sane wisdom, from which the modern reader, whatever his religious commitment or lack of it, can profit.

Ash Wednesday 2000
James Hogg
University of Salzburg

ALPHA AND OMEGA

Alpha and Omega

(musings in last hours of Millennium)

When I behold the sky and whence it came,
Ere moments were, ere stirred dazed Chronos' eyes,
Ere Void had yawned or e'er were giv'n a name,
Or stars first winked across the ancient skies,
Then well I hear the spheres in music high
Upon a yesteryear, a yesterhour
The ways of light yet trav'ling, for here I
Behold the rays once sent by Day's stray pow'r.
And there, 'yond Lethe's fondling of old Time
Long set to rest, some blest soft hours to come
Await, awake, for but a little chime
Whereat the all shall rock and call us home.
For but a point of ticking shall yet bid
Upon a clap to trap aye aught Time did.

Here begins the end

(Could you take the novitiate?)

O pain upon the bliss that hurts and hurts
To know that 'twill not come! O home not found
'Mid Sisters of an hour! O phrase that blurts
A life unmade in but a brittle sound!
High charge of highest majesty, come nigh
And mar the æons with what shall not be!
For, Master, Thine's my will, but still a sigh
I ill withhold where bold a virgin's plea.
To love we're born, and, though forlorn I hide
From noise that must abide, I see that Thou
Wouldst have me hide not maidens from the tide
Of emptiness on earth, but mirth bestowIn loving in
Thy name, the same, the same,
Some unfledged angels that e'en hither came.

2/3

Fire

(Bleeding and burning Host)

O! sight upon the night of human kind,
That saw too well to see, that passed this by
'Neath ecstasy grown great, nay, greatly blind
To particles of Bliss wherein ran high
The energies unknown... Aha! here shown
Is what came nigh upon a day wherein
The Master took my hand – here stands full shown
The matter that soft muttering within
Doth cancel from the cosmos and drive hence
To form a throne for Glory: gory pain
In white of fire, love incandescent, tense
With Being hugely here, again, again
Performs a ghostly trickery, and plays
A game forgot e'en by high technic rays.

6/5
(after seeing video of miraculous Host
venerated in Augustinian convent,
Los Teques, Venezuela.)

Fuerunt

Upon a day there hangs a day or two
Not made of time, but of long hours gone by
That linger yet, for set in fading hue
Of pigment and of pen, the moments high
But once upon the cosmos where they moved
Are true again a while, a little while,
For though no heart beat yet where these once loved,
There hovers mystery upon a smile.
O faces of our yesterday, what knew
The placid grin that thus withstands the age
That set where your sun set, and what was true
But once in time, that for all time a page
Holds firm for man's long puzzling – what aye more
Remains of pains and ecstasies of yore?

4/9
(Castiglione della Pescaia)

O purity!

Had I but known how much a nun could mean,
Would I so soon have passed these heavy walls
That hold such mystery? Had I but seen
In catching two glimpsed eyes, what gentle calls
That never found a voice could travel yet
From depth of an abyss where none e'er came
To stir a maiden yearn, would I have let
My hand yet draw the softness of name?
O flickering scintilla kindled still
Where God and man both meet, O virgin spark
Ignited by His priest, release the will
That binds this heavy chain, for e'en the dark
Can mark thee not, my angel, nor shall I
Dare tread to harm what charmed Another's eye.

L'ho visto

O pious soul, the whole of human kind
Upon thy suff'ring drew, for Calvary
In thee stood o'er the world, and in thy mind
The sins here unconfessed glared merrily.
And 'yond the tombèd years thy vision still
In glory's bosom seers each plaintive breast
That on thee cries, for skies here bend at will
At thy fond asking, hard by Godhead pressed.
O phantom not at rest, blest ghost not made
Of spectred vagabondage seeking prayer,
But coming here withal, thou canst not fade
As quickly as thy years, but standing there
In perfumed gloriole, thou teachest me
How at this grille to see, how all to see.

6/9
(San Quirico, confessing for hours)
Pious soul: Blessed Padre Pio appeared last year to one quite
normal lady, quite unexpectedly. On the anniversaryof the
occurrence, he gave another sign – a cross of light.

She died without the sacraments

(Funeral Mass at Seggiano: none called in time, that she might be shriven first.)

There hovers heavy mystery above
A bier that here we set for e'er at rest.
Alas, alas, a molecule of love
In early days held days, all days, unblest.
None called in time, timed soul, and none was there
With stole and pow'r to steal from stolen years
The matter of a worry ling'ring e'er
Upon a coffin sealed with heavy fears.
O pow'r of sound of tickings untoward
That onward o'er long æons ever go
And backward may not walk! O! moments hard
In which were marred a million – but to know,
Hid soul, the whole in time, 'twould have timed all
In fregatura high all Hell t'appal.

9/9

Hæc gloria est omnibus sanctis eius

O volume that I wind and seal at last,
O rotula with many souls enrolled,
Each merry one eternity to blast
With glory high by one shy story told:
'Tis dense with commas and full periods marked
Upon the map of Chronos where no man
May trespass or undo an æon sparked
By pain and gain that demons all did fan.
Fly high, my brethren; call where gazing faints,
For though I know a fondness that hath fear
To let all go but God, the plod of Saints
From dust to stardust conquered draws me near,
And I shall yield this morsel, this last sigh,
If fondness unto madness may draw nigh.

9/9
(completing years' work on Martyrology)

Two tombs

Two hollows side by side where morrows long
Commence their onward journey, ne'er to cease,
In parallel, in Hell or Heav'n; in song
Or howling o'er long harrowing; in peace
Or wanting but a moment evermore,
For that no priest did come – no priest like this
That calmly shut his eyes upon this store
Of moments weighed and gathered unto bliss...
O! mystery where history lies still
In characters indelible upon
The book of all that live – O! flick of Will
That will or will not go where all have gone
But only did they will, for till the end,
That end ne'er can, a man no hour may mend.

10/9
(at 3.00 a.m., concerned for the lady at Seggiano, whom we
buried next to a faithful priest friend.)

O Thing!

O Thing that has no name, O Mystery
Beyond the yonder land where all is well
Or not so well, where ancient History
Is long in its unwriting, Heav'n and Hell
Upon a moment pending, vending all
In calling Will that still could turn the tide
Of æons ere they came and e'er went on
Upon a tracèd course high bound and tied
Unto a distant second ever gone –
O Thing without a name, whose fame is bright
In regions where no sight may penetrate,
I spent some moons a-roving in thy light
Unveiled and hailed afar, for at this gate
Upon a manuscript I pored awhile
And heard a noisèd land where demons smile.

30/9
Manuscript: The letter from Hell and the Purgatory
Manuscript, translated in France. (Cf. Ave Maria Press,
Middletown, Co. Armagh.)

Lines jotted after seeing a surprise sketch

(of my face, drawn during conference)

A picture is a drop of flowing time
Made still and, once distilled, left eíer to dry
While onward calls the voice of every chime
That never stopped to stay, but, standing high
Above the world, hurled hours to where they go
Beyond, beyond where yonder moments are
Awaiting our return, and seconds flow
Too quickly where we are, for there afar
Our home awaits our coming, for not here
Are we long meant to be. We are alone
Suspended ítween two hours, and very near
Is ancient patient rest to what was known
By every passing soul for aye and aye
There where the seconds lie and ever stay.

2002
(Vatican)

After seeing pictures
(of my cell at Sélignac)

A picture fossils ticks of clappèd time
Twice tapped within the heart, a part of us
That came this way before, an ancient crime
That cannot be undone, a moment thus
Once spent and ever bent on being all
That evermore shall be ñ a drop that lies
Embedded on a sheet that eíer shall call
The shape of many morrows íneath the skies.
O cell, O happy hell where all was known,
Will this thy door yet open for a child
That weighed not well a blessing, where a groan
Too heavy for a heart did moments wild
With consequences fashion merrily,
Without a thought for years no more to be?

19-20/6/02
(on the occasion of the feast of St Romuald)

12

After sending a letter to Fr Winfried

Fly, letter, home, and gently call upon
The heart that shall thee hear, for here at hand
Is Paradise, and coming here anon
Are days that can days mend and ever stand
In altered form upon the page unwrit
That History shall form and mightily
Shall seal as sealed were hours and days by it
Upon a day that wrote eternally.
O powír of but an hour, of but a page
Swift scribbled íneath the sun, do well thy task
And change the form of growing and of age
By granting this small mercy that I ask:
A place to be, a place to be again
Alone, alone with Lonelinessí soft pain.

19-20/6/02

13

A warning

A little at a time, a little more
Fidelity to what one yesterday
Was laid in holocaust for eíer before
The eyes of Majesty, for here to stay
Are hours for ever offered, and the gaze
The looked upon the paten that here bore
The sacrifice on high, for all my days
Still reads and heeds its echo evermoreÖ
To be a victim on this altar placed,
And not upon another, this is all
My heritage on earth, for I have traced,
In syllables well heard, the morrowís call.
And though a distant cell calls well, too well,
I have been warned that calls call oft from Hell.

16/7/03

A week in the Order

To found another house where there is peace
And rest from all that weighs, from many things
That need not be, that could an instant cease
To be the burden that for ever clings
To ones not made for this, to ones not bound
To bear the whole worldís weight ñ to build anew
A desert as of old where once was found
The sound of silence that Prémontré knew ñ
To be alone with friends in hallowed space
íNeath Norbertís ancient sign, and to be Thine
As once the novice was, in but a place
Enough for simple praise:ítwould be to shine
Before a Monstrance bright, and bid yet be
A mighty sin that could bid new saints be.

7/8/03
 (after being at Frigolet)

Glimmer

(after two talks with the Prior)

A word, a mighty word, herein was heard,
And now the morrow can again be fair:
A little hope in this small sound well stirred
The deadened heart that nothing more could bear.
A day may come when this same powír that barred
The way to solitude may say the word
That bids me cross again the æons marred
And walk again the land that error blurred.
O Erin, come again and be my home,
Not formed of flagrant sin and rupture made
With all that once was vowed ñ nay, bid me come
And shelter from the blast in this vast shade
Of faith that stands upon a land I know,
That knows me well, that bids me homeward go.

Venite seorsum

O angels made of matter not of earth
Or human clay defined, O flames of fire
Lit by the ancient Sun, whose gentle mirth
Beams in your virgin gaze, what calm desire
Not made of man's embrace here draws you on
To fondling of a soul where spirits walk
Alone upon a land wherein is done
A work of which no tongue may ever talk?
Come close to this gold vessel where the all
Meets in a soft Amen, and then return
To this strange grille that hides the matters small
That are the all of living; let me burn
Awhile 'neath this your smiling, for there are
Some looks that travel hither from afar.

28/9
(after Verona)

Half a century

(in the Norbertine habit)

A day, another day, a year,
A year again, another yet again,
A moment where a century is near,
For that it knows the weight of years to gain ñ
This is the all of passing, this is all
The weight of this our matter: we move on
Upon the little patter of a call
Oft heard by pilgrims of a journey done.
Move on, fair soul, and walk the years that hold
Thy moments yet in poise, for noise for long
We cannot make or leave, and rhythms old
Shall measure yet the tapping of our song.
The morrow comes, the morrow goes its way,
And none can tread for long upon a day.

13/10
(For the Prior)

Spiritual direction

My sisters, my dear sisters, is this true
That for a while the gentle, gentle weight
Of souls immortal, lost in regions new,
Unstudied heretofore, uncalculated fate
And Providence benign bids me now bear,
By day, by night, by prayer and touch unknown,
By word well writ and heard, by message long
In wires electric sent by one alone
Who knows aye well the language of your song?
O! instruments of man, bring woman kind
In all her beauty veiled to this chaste cell
Where heart sees well the heart, where but the mind
Emits an angel's burden captured well.
eyes, I see you all –
All, all, I say, in unsaid signals small.

27/6/4
(eve of feast of Bd. Paul Giustiniani)

19

Gladness

And I had thought that there could never be
A presence in the world beside thine own,
My Lord, my precious Lord: Eternity
Seemed long in its aloneness, all alone
Beyond the realm of loving, feeling aught
But what may not be felt. I thought not
That e'er again a message might be caught
From depths of the within e'ermore forgot.
My Love, I knew not love could yet be known
There where the flesh moves not, from where
naught moves
But undefiled deep movements. Yet alone
I know I ne'er shall be. Henceforth two loves
Made all of Thee, have made of three one whole,
For by thy touch here touch two gleams of soul.

Canities

When in the end the years begin to bend
Towards their old beginning, when we are
Alone upon a cosmos, that doth send
A little light for living 'neath a star
That shone for others too, that onward went
Along a lonely road that held us not
For long, for very long, for song was sent
By other cords like ours ere soon forgot.
We hurry on our way, for Yesterday
Is longer than the Morrow in its sleep
Upon the pages that record our way.
For yet a day or two and we shall peep
Beyond these stars that hide the very all
That is and ever was beyond recall.

23/8/05
(for the Prior)

Deduxit eos in montem altum seorsum

Will this yet come again, will we yet be
Alone together, yet all all alone
To do but little, there where two or three
Have One there in their midst, as if their own,
Here calling some apart, not much to do,
But only to but be, there where He wills
That they be there with Him, that they be true
To one, one only love that time all fills?
Aha! A time apart, all time apart
To spend long whiles a-gazing, this I hear
Thou wouldst me give, for in the human heart
There lies a sigh where Godhead would draw near.
And I behold upon this mountain white
A beauty known, well known, where youth was
bright.

24/11/05
(in retreat, Sisters of Bethlehem)

22

Rumania

(after news of unanimous chapter vote)

A *Sì* is but a noise, but makes a noise
That travels over lands that kept two hands
That held awhile then left the world in poise
'Tween what was thought and what for ever stands
Upon a page of Time to be well writ
And in a place to be, and in a world
To have a right to palpitate where it
Knows but to hurt in very Hell unfurled.
O gentle Sisters, come and rest awhile
In this the nest where loving is well known
To be of little done, for but a smile
Did gladden all the world, and God shall own
A corner of this globe where there shall be
No room for harm, for God pronounced this *Sì*.

23/1/6

Little light

There is a place where I can pose my soul
And rest betimes where times are heavy borne;
There is a part wherein e'ermore the whole
Of what I am lives here no more forlorn.
There is a presence in the universe
Where void may no more be, there is yet heat
Within the cosmos vast where I immerse
The sorrows that none knew: nay, little feet
That travel from afar bring many things
Within a corpulet, and in a breast
A warmth heals many years, and even wings
Of soul that cannot come make yet their nest
'Cross miles that are no more, where more is known
Of owning than much breath would ever own.

26/2

Lasciarsi amare è amore non meno che amare

What 'tis to know that when the world is dar-
kAnd home was never found, for it came not,
There is an ear that did the beating hark
Of one small heart that others had forgot;
That 'cross the miles and walls that firmly hold
Two worlds in poise – the one of noise oft heard
In chambers of hard learning things of old,
And th'other of long waiting for a word –
And that there is a head that all things knows
That need be known on earth, then in the din
Of many hollow sounds a something glows
Across the cosmos bare, for 'tis not sin
To let another know that one has heard
What needed not the channel of a word.

27/3
Lasciarsi...: Quotation taken from daily Franciscan text
sent out over Italy via Internet, and sent on with many
others by Rosa.

A year

(from the proposal of a foundation)

To rest upon a breast that none e'er saw
And know that there is peace yet upon earth
Far from the raging blast, at last before
The gates of Gladness where some spark of mirth
Not made of Sense, but denser still; to hide
From cosmic Cold in scarce a hold where all
Was known, alone where lonely æons sighed:
This is to feel, where feeling could not be,
A being that none felt, a melting well
Of matter made of soul, a whole set free
To rest within a nest where damnèd Hell
Dared not e'en raise its head, for naught was said
In Silence that healed violence where two bled.

2/4
(anniversary of Holy Father's death)

Tu ci sei

What 'tis to know that there is someone there
Upon the night yet lying, not afar
But on a moment shared, there only where
One other knows the way, where none may mar
The place that on the breast of God was found,
For that he bled for this, and left a word
That named His own in but a little sound
That ages oft at this same Altar heard...
A God is bold in love, and shall we be
Afraid to hold the flame that bid us come
Upon a night from Night, this light to see
Where here the rays that made us call us home?
O Sister, let me rest on this thy breast
Not made of thee, made of strange magic blest.

20/4
(keeping vigil)

Hortus conclusus

And I thought not that ever would there be
A place in one for two, a place to lie
Within where yet without all Hell set free
Did rage with foulest din, there where a sigh
That none e'er heard did rock the cosmos whole,
And I knew not of regions where no man
Had dared unshod to tread, where soul and soul
Did stand alone and touch as flesh ne'er can.
I knew not of a place where space was not
'Tween thought and thought, where nought
neede'en be said,
Where in a world of men was long forgot
The knowing of a wanting where one bled.
And I thought not that I would know again
A land not made of hurting and of pain.

Virgin

What 'tis to tread where man has never trod
And gaze upon a soul that never held
Another in its hearth, where only God
Did enter in, to see what none beheld
And to hear all that never could be said
By one that could not speak where none could hear,
And by a gaze to be but sweetly led
To regions where some mighty things drew near:
'Tis to be on a planet where the air
An ether not of earth sends to and fro,
For in a word a very being bare
I contemplate and, holding close, well know.
For many men well wed walk on alone,
While something strange bid virgins virgins own.

Mystery

It is a strange, strange thing to know a soul
And hear what ne'er was known, and stranger still
In half a sound unmade the very whole
Of chasmèd hollows vast, that ne'er a thrill
Had hitherto disturbed, to penetrate
And resonating hear, for near the core
Of what another is there is a gate
Whose sigils high none ever broke before.
And I thought not that I would ever see
Within an eye, the window wherein all
Unsaid was calmly read, that parts of me
Moved in another breast, that something small
For which the world cared not, was all to one
In whose fond gaze soft rays of healing shone.

Time

O Master, stop the world, for there is time
To lie awhile where moments have their weight
And live twice o'er, for Mem'ry's heavy chime
One hour to hours to come will yet relate.
O moments loaded with such heavy things,
You were not made to pass; cast here awhile
In Chronos' sea your anchor, there where clings
Unto a second gone a once known smile.
We have not pow'r to hold the hours that were
A second time not made, but fading die
As this the sun that roused them, yet they stir
From this their bygone being oft a sigh.
For there was gladness once or twice untold,
And two that held at whiles hold long their hold.

**You may be only one person in the world,
but you may also be the world to one person**

An ant moves on alone and is not seen,
And underfoot is trod: without a name
It is no more as it had never been,
And something that was not it shall remain.
But there is in the web of days an hour
That evermore shall be, and one alone
Can rock the universe with strangest pow'r
For that no other cared the stray to own.
A moment known by two long moments knows
'Tween Solitude's high walls, and something calls,
E'en from the slumbered night, that yet bestows
A tingle of a touch that Home recalls.
For Home is where a breast made room for me,
And to be needed is to be bid be.

The Vatican's majestic walls

(Congregation for Religious)

Eight years have passed and more since last herein
I walked and talked with pow'rs that moved the
world;
Eight years, I say, and more have passed, wherein
I too have walked the regions where are hurled
The forces of the world in wildest flight,
For I have trodden lands where no man walks
And I have gazed at Vision that no sight
Of naked eye can see. No demon gawks
Where I have watched and heard, no angel treads
Where virgins bid me stand. I have heard all
Within an eye that beamed, and little heads
That held the cosmos whole to me did call
To come this way and say what need be said
That virgins may have love and be twice wed.

27/5
(Written in retreat, San Nazario, 30/5)

The rape of the lock

(Would you cut my hair?)

And I thought not that I would clip the locks
Of brides of Christ flown hither for to nest.
These little sighs in which the cosmos rocks
Bid me hold wide my breast and let here rest
At last these bits of soul: the whole is played
Upon the clipping sound that cuts the past
From this great gambled hour. In hairs are
weighed
The years e'ermore o'ergrown. A sound doth blast
The ticket never used, the home bid be
A morsel in the mind. Behind is all
The web of Atropos. Eternity
Hangs on a fibre snipped. A current small
Trims ever ever more an order sound,
For this small head that bled some healing found.

2/6

34

An old familiar smile

Will this yet be, my Sister, will this be,
That we upon a while shall be alone -
Alone, alone, I say, and merrily
The healing wings of glory softly own
And over others cast – the blast of Hell
Shall we in Song outdo in basking long
There where no Haste need be: the ling'ring smell
Of burning Prayer, shall it draw hours along
To chasmèd Waste, to utterness of Loss,
To Folly of all kinds, where kindness means
The meaning of a day, where one small Host
Warms all for evermore? Tomorrow gleans
In this brief sigh I heard the means to be,
For what a will shall will writes History.

18/7

Fons signatus

When in the night the dark is doubly dark
And nothing moves where no one ever came,
When 'neath the stars a yearn soft whispers,
"Hark,
Hark yet, hark well the meaning of a name," –
When there is distance none 'tween distant parts
But only rest of wanting nought to be
But clinging soul and soul, – then broken hearts
In one short hour create eternity.
For there are sparks within that wield the world
And two at times know all that need be known.
To touch upon a need is to be hurled
Into a universe that none did own.
And though no touch may be where none may
move,
There is a knowing none but virgins prove.

Ecclesiastes

(chapter 3, verse 5)

There is a time to touch, a time to hold;
A time no more to cling, no more to be
Another upon earth: the mirth too bold
Of Yesterday tomorrow shall not see
Where whiles perhaps should never here have
been
Upon our pages writ. Yet we bear all
The weight of what was known and what was
seen
Where meanings have no words, but ripples small
Of soul and touching soul, for aye we gaze
Upon the stagèd moments where we were,
And there is coming back from where lost days
Once shone, no, never none, for one soft stir
Stirs for all time e'en when 'tis no more ours
To touch again the pulse of touching hours.

Letter from a bishop

Upon a page an age doth calmly shine,
And in a sound the bounds of Heav'n and Hell
Are into orbit hurled, for it is Thine
To call upon the calling of this bell
That long in silence lay: a day can dawn
Again again upon our ancient land,
And sacred sound can hallow yet the morn,
If giv'n it be on Gwalia yet to stand.
I hear in accents fond the sound of peace,
And Grace may pass again in Song our own.
If this be giv'n, much pain long known may cease
Upon a line or two of meaning shown.
For in these lines I hear the sound of Home,
And mighty letters o'er the seas bid, "Come!".

12/8
A bishop: Anglican bishop of Bangor, who is keen to
have a Welsh house of prayer.

Sunt lacrimæ rerum

In but a globule moves a molten soul,
And words have not a sound, but only form.
A heaviness too great at times may roll
In molecules of womanhood yet warm
With what we are, for in a liquid sound
Is seen and heard what never can be said,
And oft a yearn a softer voice here found
And more obtained than mightiness ill led.
For depth calls on a depth, and there are things
That need no more be said, and hearing lies
Not in the ear, but here where being clings
To being that knows all. For unheard sighs
Are heard by two alone when travels all
Upon a bathèd furrow weak and small.

Opening packet

(of printed volumes)

What lies upon the page no eye can tell,
And morrows yet to come a sorrow gone
Perchance may hear again, for knowing well
What once a moment held, when once there shone
A sun that came and went, we can again
Draw tears from eyes unseen, for some great things
In other bosoms lie, and oft a pain
Is deeper than a joy that too well sings.
And yet there is a tingle where was mirth,
And Yesterday shines on 'fore these same eyes
That saw these squiggles come, and all the earth
In long siesta yawns, for patient skies
Unchanged look down upon a range of days
That evermore shall be, where move these rays.

24/8

Vox dilecti

A cell of hearing matter can afford
A molecule of touch across the air
Where touching may not be, and but a word
May breast and breast well join, for all is there
Where syllables return, and I have known
In this small face the trace of many sighs
That moved not in the air to be outblown
But came to rest again where meaning lies.
For sighs and sounds come hence, and mighty things
Join pieces of stray soul, and wholly fond
Is bosom that to bosom calmly clings
Not where a body meets, but there beyond
The heavy miles that oft at whiles are long,
For to a cell two captured yearns belong.

Homeward bound

What is a home where yet the heart doth roam
Abroad in distant hills, when ills are such
That walls re-echo all but sounds of Home
And what means all means naught that mattes much –
When there can be what here can ne'er e'r be
And all that need be known can to the tomb
Be known, nay, doubly known, when two may see
And feel and hold the warmth of Home's great womb?
For Home is where we are when we are not
By homeless hearts ill tied, when eyes behold
The all in but a sparkle, when forgot
Is all that hurts in but a sound too bold.
And even words say less than other things,
For Home is where a being softly clings.

1/9

If this fire remains alight this night, it will never go out

There is a flame a-kindled in my breast
That waits to burn again where there was mirth
In bygone days there 'neath the sleeping West
Where we began to patter on this earth –
A fire that high'r could rise and travel far
If what I hear be true, if what I see
Be seen not in the mind, where wantings mar
The vision of the sage, to demons' glee.
There is, and there can be, a mighty thing
Of ancient Pow'r enriched, if pitched be there
On Gwalia's acres fair,'neath this same Wing
That patted Dewi's cheek, this mishcief's lair
Made all of cunning plotting when no man
But God alone ignited chuckle can.

3/9
If this fire…: Druids' words regarding St Patrick's fire.

Paulinus and Therasia

Will this yet be one day, will this yet be?
The madness that made well the Saints of old,
Will it us heal? Shall we yet wake and see
A rest made of a sleep a little bold
Where soul looks into soul and sees the all
Behind a retina, a waiting eye,
A mystery unveiled in matters small
That mattered much to such as shared a sigh?
Shall we yet know what few have known below,
For that 'twas knowledge loud that many shared
That shared not silent sound and could not know
The knowledge of a being wholly bared?
We are alone save when alone alone
With nothing but another heard and known.

5/9

An altar all alone

Come, virgin, to a home where love can be
Free to be known and heard, there where the all
Is in its parts well touched, where ecstasy
In little bliss can lie, and echoes small
Can travel far within – within, I say,
For virgins meet in sound, and we have found
A rite as old as is the light of day
That with a tingle heals this trodden ground.
For rays of warmth are known when all alone
We stand beneath the Sun that calls us home
To kindly sounds and melodies well known
And altars where some mystic wings bid, "Come,
Come, come and walk again on hallowed land,
And 'neath the wind of ancient madness stand."

23/9

'Απορία

O huge and mighty Void, wherein no more
A grain of meaning stands, where lands of Sense
'Neath oceans of high Madness sink before
The puzzled gaze that watches Chaos dense
Work in an hour a pow'r that nethergloom
Ne'er dreamt it muster could! O Thing no name
Was wide enough to hold, what old foul doom
Did call thee forth and through thee Godhead
tame?
Shall I sit by and see a Nonsense plod
Upon a pattern blest, at the behest
Of one or two half-wise, and shall stars nod
At whims that rule the world? Nay, this was blest,
And shall be blest again. Bride thou shalt be,
And hold the hand that holds Eternity.

13/11
 (in retreat)

Mass alone

The heart of man is but of fibres made,
But in its beat all holds; the oldest pain
Is ever young herein, and one that played
A moment on its cords came not again
In safety from a land whereon he trod,
For to be owned, e'en for a passing hour,
Is hours e'ermore to be to stand unshod
Before a sacred burning of strange pow'r.
And yet as I here climb a step or two
That bid me stand and feel, and feel and stand
Before a Flame not felt, a feeling true
Made all of knowing well, calls from a land
That tingled oft beneath a virgin breast
And bid no soul upon a fibre rest.

14/11
(in retreat)

47

Hoc est enim ...

There hovers o'er a stone a mighty work,
And, gazing, I see all that darkened sight
Sees with a mind's high gaze, for here doth lurk
A grain or two of time that this same might
Here piercèd oft before, and soft the sound
That severs yet again the molecules
That, save at whiles, the colours t'which they're
bound
'Neath heavy Change change not: here monti-
cules
Of Reason grow insane, and pain I know
Not made of hurt, but of high chargèd rays.
And, as 'tween heart and heart the part doth
show
The whole of meaning meant, so here there plays
Upon a sparkle pow'r of deep embrace,
And God I elevate in face to face.

15/11
 (in retreat)

Sir, we desire to see the Lord

Is there a pulpit where the mighty word
In Cymric accents clear may come again
To tingle in the ear that, list'ning, heard
What oft was thought, and, hearing, bid remain
In echoes long reheard, reheard until
The morrow took new form? O! storm upon
The heads that, nodding, sleep, come, thunder, fill
The rafters with a classic din long gone.
For few the sounds of yesteryear forthtell
And demons joy to see an ancient flame outblown,
And clinic art of th'art of very Hell
In bidding it not be its whiles well own.
For souls anæsthetized drop blissfully
Into a pit thought oft no more to be.

16/11
(in retreat)

All

There is a corner of the earth, but one,
Where I am king and hold a little sway,
And more I do in leaving well undone
Such as may well not be, for none did say,
"Do this and this", for bliss in pressure high
Came rarely to a soul, and to be whole
Is to be all at one, and eye to eye
Much more is known and heard 'tween soul and soul.
And Thou, my King, hast not said anything
Of sound and boundless bustling, nay, thy word
Is made of soft embrace, for virgins cling
But only in the dark, where all is heard.
And virgin shall I be, for Thee, for Thee,
For too much heat can mar Eternity.

18/11
 (end of retreat)

Liturgy

There is a pain upon the Cosmos vast,
A suff'ring harsh that hardens all that is.
A place no more there is wherein at last
A touch may yet be known, for that 'tis His,
And felt as such to be, where human kind
Is not the all of all: there is no more
An echo of the vast unheard, where mind
Is glad at last to puzzle, where before
Long ages happy were nought here to know,
But only taste and see – there is no time
To stand upon a cloud and ponder how
A myriad days were lost in one fell chime.
There is a place for mystic magic yet,
And wasted moments oft all Time reset.

14/12

Veni, dilecta

(Lauds 'neath angels guardian)

A word once heard rests long upon the ear
And heart that it received, perceived to be
A part of all unsaid, and two brought near
By currrents in the air, there mightily
Do much where such soft prayer 'neath other skies
Ignited never knew, for two know all
That in twinned hearts can stir where muffled sighs
In psalmic sounds entwined on Heaven call.
For melody of beauty is a part,
But th'all is greater still, and prayer alive
Upon the clouds pounds hard there where the art
Of neums not muttered well, for there arrive
Two angels in the midst where we alone
Alone less never were, the all to own.

Beyond

Upon the night there trembles in the dark
A light not known, a presence yet well known,
And there where comes not sleep, peeps yet the
spark
Of soul and nearing soul that bids it own.
Alone we walk not here when we are seen
Not by the gazing eye, the touch too fond,
But by the mem'ry held of where have been
Some moments shared in sacred lands, beyond.
Beyond, beyond where retina sees not,
A beauty was once was seen where simple things
Knew more of bliss and ecstasy forgot
Than pulsèd magic where no matter clings.
For matter matters little to the soul
That in a retina saw once the whole.

Too much

There is a pow'r that rules the universe,
A word unheard that continents divides,
A moment that no moments may reverse
Or bid ne'er to have been, a place where hides
The forces that made Hell or Paradise,
For one soft word holds cosmic dazings long,
And oft a soul that heard it wrecked the skies
Of glory that were his, for one brief song.
We are not well when things too heavy move
Beneath the skies that made us, we are not
For shocks of this size measured: here to prove
What made the very soul is e'er to rot
Upon a bliss too great, or here to be
Called unto pain that gained eternity.

10/1/7

Telefonino

To hold a little thing is to hold all
That travels in the air from breast to breast.
To wait upon the dark upon a call
From distant light is safely here to nest
Within a fondness known, and to see well
Behind two eyes unseen a cosmos vast
Of History unsaid, of hours to tell
To ne'er a soul on earth unto the last.
For moments come and go that none may own
Save those alone to whom apart they came.
And unto eyes that met huge vistas shown
Forbade all time to be, to be the same.
And I have rest upon a little thing
Wherein without a cord two hearts hard cling.

16/1

Children

(Luke 18, 15)

There come at whiles some smiles from yesterday,
And feelings no more known know yet to be
Known deeply where they were, for gone away
Are hours that rocked awhile Eternity.
To hold a bundle bold that merrily
Within no signal keeps but says well all
In calories that move, and privily
To sense upon a tremble something call
From depth to depth, abyss to deep abyss
There where a wanting is in clinging said,
Is to have captured rayons of a bliss
That nested in the rest of one small head.
Where are the little fondles that did lie
'Neath fastened eyes, upon a half-heard sigh?

16/1
(singing to Annalisa)

Power to touch

There is a beauty that no eye did see,
A splendour e'er so fair that nothing saw
Its glister 'neath the sun: a sound can be
A tremour in the sky, and heat can thaw
The glaciers of long age, but there are rays
That pierce the sinews of the dormant soul
And messages that cervic matter daze
When in a glimpse the Vision all was whole.
The poundings of the organs loud made strong
Heard not the murmur of a softer bliss,
And rhythmic rumblings of the wildest song
Knew not a tear as sweet as sound like this.
For I perceive that Beauty is not made
Of heaviness, but meaning heavy-laid.

17/1

Consecration

O Master, call again, for I Thee hear
Upon the æons pulling from afar,
And in these red drops lying, lying near
The breast that hosts thy coming, there where are
Too many matters moving, thou dost stir
The heart that Thou dost enter, and bid come,
Come home to where Thou art, to where we were
Upon a blessing one, where void was Home.
O Master, homeward-bound I'd be again
There were soft music plays that long was heard
'Tween wall and wall where called a sweetest pain
To nought but sounds of silence where there stirred
Enough for one to be and not to be,
Enough for one to call what called on me.

17/1

Bimba

Press not so hard, my little little friend,
And hold not him that holds thee, for far more
Is known where nothing moves and no pow'rs lend
Stray energies in vain: to be before
A place of much great warmth, and there to stir
Not even in a fibre, 'tis to rest
In blissful rest of old, to lie where were
The hours long missed, the sacred minutes pressed.
There is a place to be a part of one
That did not hurt in heat, for heat came not
To harm an angel's slumber, and thereon
Much in an hour was known of hours forgot.
For 'neath the sun some moments pass this way
That need not e'er have been, yet shall be, aye.

18/1

Kindness

There are yet corners in the universe
Where unknown angels hide, there are yet eyes
That hide a world undreamt, and, where e'er worse
Is human kind on earth, the darkened skies
At whiles left soft rays peep: nay, I have seen
Upon a face a world, a land unthought
To be again allowed; nay, I have been
Too close to angel wings, and have been caught.
O maid, who made thee thus, and kept thee so
Untouched by aught of earth? O little thing,
Whence came these angel twinkles that yet know
To singe a soul and bid a glimmer cling?
O cherub never known, who turned my feet
To find all Heav'n all hid 'hind one more street?

18/1
(Marcellina)

Demons in the air

Ten years have passed since passed in but a touch
The pow'r of logic old, the Logos all,
Into a little head – a tingle such
That æons made here tingled in a call
Of apostolic magic and bid be
A word on word of healing, for herein
A tongue was doubly loosed – eternity
Did travel in the tremble of a din,
And nethergloom perceived that 'twas not well,
The mingling of this sound, and pounded oft
On gadgets and on brains, for very Hell,
On hearing it much mentioned, wilings soft
At whiles would send to bend the currents high
Lest aught be heard of damnèd æons nigh.

25/1

Cistercium mater nostra

There is a place where I may rest my soul
Beyond the storm where warms satanic glee,
And in a word is heard the very whole
Of what in but a nod could ever be.
I see, I see a path where armies vast
O'er Time have trampled well and homeward gone,
And on this day another day long passed
I see dawn yet where youth's fair rays once shone.
O Cîteaux, come again and give me birth
In this thy virgin womb where secret things
Once whispered in the ear, when all the earth
Knew only of one love, for Silence sings
More loudly than the world where hearts meet not,
And but a word holds echoes long forgot.

14/2
(reflecting on pressing invitation of Abbadia monks)

Hail, emerald isle

(The power of a text)

And I thought not that I would see again
The acres green where grace worked well on me
'Tween storm and storm, 'tween pain and aching
pain,
Where time its trace in trodden history
Left ever evermore – these gentle eyes
As blue as this deep sea bid once Goodbye
And bid me come again 'cross these same skies
By dint of engines technic madly high.
O Erin, come to view and call me home
To simple things, to warmth made not of woe...
Alas the day that dawned and bid me roam
From goodness of a kind few kindreds know.
Alas, alas, we travel hurriedly
O'er moments offered once and bid not be.

3/3
(sailing out of Holyhead)

Many people will walk in and out of your life, but only true friends will leave footprints in your heart

There is on earth a mirth that heals the soul,
A merriment not measured in its grin.
There is a hearth wherein is known the whole
Of ancient joy without the toy of sin.
There is a place far from all human kind
Where kindness is the all, there is a land
Where madness is but sane, where years behind
The race of æons new have time to stand.
There is, there will be yet, a place to be
Unmasked and all well known where all is known
In fondness of true smiles – there is for me
A place to be but me, where little things
In th'engrenage were caught, where something
clings.

4/3
(Athboy)

Il nostro desiderio

*(è di creare una famiglia dove ci sarà molto amore, e
solo amore)*

There is much hurt upon the planet Earth
And many tears unheard that stars see well,
There are some corners where no longer mirth
May e'en in snippets come, where hell to hell
Through long osmosis seeps and keeps the all
In absence of all fondness firmly bound,
And there are dwellings where from wall to wall
There travel heavy echoes of hard sound.
But there is yet a place where we can be
Alone with Fondness gazing from on high,
A tent of meeting where hid Eyes may see
What travels in the language of a sigh.
There is a place where space can hold desire
Not to possess but to caress pure fire.

14/3
(Wales, replying to Annalisa)

My children, why do you hurry so?

(asked Jesus through a chosen soul)

There is no time to live a moment well,
And many hours were marred when laden more
Than they did need to be: the ancient bell
That calmly chimed our days called not before
To tugging at the pendulum that sways
Unhurried o'er our haste, and waste was not
A moment overspent, for many days
Were fairer 'neath a merriment forgot.
The air bears messages where one or two
Sufficed in yesteryear, and we vibrate
To currents multiplied, and piercèd through
Are little heads that evermore rotate.
There is a time to be, but 'tis not made
Of much as such as need not be obeyed.

A chosen soul: a lay apostle through whom He goes on
to speak in the same vein (by inner locution), as follows:
"Why do you feel you must move so quickly through
your days? This is not the way I intended the children of
God to live. You may tell Me that you have many things
to do. I respond to you by saying that you are trying
to do too much. You will not be holy if you move so
quickly."

Sgwrs

(gyda Gwyn Erfyl)

Y mae i bethau cu eu bregys wedd,
Ac nid oes yma aros lle na fydd
Yfory'n eiddo in. Y mae i hedd
Ei drigfan yn ein plith, ond trigfan sydd
Yn drom ei gosteg faith: y daith fydd hir,
Ond eto ryfedd fer, lle nad oes iaith
I adrodd eto'r ffordd, a'r pethau gwir
A guddiwyd hyd yn hyn gânt hanes maith.
Ac eiliad na ddaw'n ôl ddaw byth yn ôl
I'r cof ysigwyd yma, a'r fan draw
Yng nghof pechadur trist a thystion ffôl
A roddodd oll am hyn o 'fory ddaw.
Cans dyfod wna, a myned y mae'r oll
A fu yn gu i ni ar orig goll.

17/3

Ἅγιὸς ἰσχυρὸς

Dio Padre, Creatore,
Dio santo, forte, Re,
Dio immortale, buono,
Nel tempio del mio
Sei Re.

Gesù, mio Redentore,
Gesù, mio Salvator,
Sei tu Verbo che risuoni
Nel tempio del mio cuor
Dal ciel.

Amor e Vita, vieni,
O vieni, Creator,
E prendi qui il tuo trono
Nel tempio del mio cuor
D'amor.

(Melody: *Be still and know I am near you*)

Remember, friend, as you pass by

*(As you are now, so once was I, As I am now, you will
also be, So prepare yourself to follow me.)*

There is yet time to stand upon a rhyme
And look upon the moments yet to be.
There is a stillness 'tween each heavy chime
That holds its clap at bay, for History
Has pow'r to be rewrit ere it be born,
And moments over moments have a say
Ere they join others 'neath a burnèd dawn
That came and went as but a heedless day.
O Master of the Chronicle unseen,
Unread, unheard, what word dost Thou discern?
And what small causèd cause shall once have
been
The cause of archives æons aye shall learn?
We splash an hour or two upon this pond,
And ripples go for e'er to the Beyond.

26/3
(after reading gravestone at Gellilydan)

Il Maestro è qui, e ti chiama

There is a place to be, and doubly be,
A home where we can come and be alone
Away from what can wait, where we can see
The gaze that bid us come, where we can own
Both Thee and what we know, for we know more
'Tween souls that cling than many souls apart
E'en held by holds too hard, e'en should the door
Of all be opened wide, yet but in part.
For all is known not where the flame is strong
In loudness of high heat, and meeting here
Is made of matter such as can belong
Not to a fragile bliss – for some are near
To where they are not when there is too much –
But of a gaze amazed at what did touch.

28/3

Betania

I thought not, sister, that 'twould come to this,
That vanity of looks thus peeled away
'Neath such strange hands would fall, or that I'd
miss
The sound of this sweet shearing, where the day
Heard humming and soft play, where little things
Meant much to little souls, where gladness hid
At whiles may smile upon the heart that sings
Content to see thus spent what madness bid.
Keep this wee lock in th'envelope that days
Perhaps again shall find, and mind the hour
That heard thy cherub tune, for sweetness plays
With mildness of its own, of wildest pow'r.
And 'tis enough to know, to know but this,
That there is gladness in a little bliss.

29/3

Psalm 132 [131], 14

To want is to be there where there is not
But what alone may be; to will 'tis to be ill,
For that the all high called could not be got
And that the mind yet owned could not be still.
To gaze on what comes not, and not to see
The fairness of what is, 'tis not to hold
The bliss that we may touch; 'tis not to be
Alert to half a word a little bold.
And I perceive that much was lost on earth
By pressing hard where softness was full well,
And that a spark was oft a greater mirth
Than magic high enkindled in nigh Hell.
And there's a place where wanting may find rest,
For th'utmost was not always what was best.

30/3

Absolute solitude

(for discernment)

To be alone again is to be well
With hills unchanged that knew of ancient days,
With sounds oft found ere pounding of high Hell
Bid man his hours o'erpow'r and madly daze.
To be alone and hear what near the soul
May come again when other voices cease,
To dare upon a frenzied hour to stroll
And hear in hurry huge the æons' peace:
This is to linger where a better time
May tick o'er damnèd heads, this is to be
Not hammered 'neath a space 'tween chime and
chime,
But yet alone with ancient melody.
And if 'tis thus, I'll bid this silence come
To other breasts in but a simple home.

4/4
(Abersoch)

If music be the food of love ...

O Master, bid this be, bid this bliss be
Our part upon this globe: plant here thy tent
There where love will Thee hide, where two or three
May hold Thee in the midst, where sounds all meant
May reach thy Godhead's ears, where Beauty high
May be thine earthly home, where healing wings
May touch a soul that could perchance draw nigh
To magic old that clings to plainest things.
To be so close, 'twould be to hear again
A heartbeat heard before, and be alone
With all that matters in a world of pain
That for a softer beauty oft did grown.
For height of sound that pounded in the air
Neared Godhead less than hearing Godhead there.

5/4
(Holy Thursday, in solitude)

Utter goodness

A brother is another one of us
Of membranes like and chromosomes well
known.
For I perceive that to be counted thus
Is giv'n to none but unto such that own
A part of what they are, 'neath features theirs,
'Neath sounds and sayings fond that are the all
Of what they ever knew, for brother bears
The weight of little brother ever small.
And there are days that show where home still
lies
'Cross continents unlike, and there are hours
That tell of bondings known where childhood dies
Not as the morn that bore it: there are pow'rs
Of Goodness hid where no high technic art
Of godliness bid goodliness depart.

24/4
(Pwllheli)

75

The old place

(in the library)

When we return to where turned once the all
That could have been, when seen 'neath these
same skies
Are little things too great, when wall and wall
Hold yesterday in poise, when fondest eyes
Come not again the pain of waiting long
To still in their appearing, when no more
The sound of gentle words, the mingled song
Of voices wed come hither as before,
Then there is in a scent sent from the past
A hugeness of long wanting, there is touch
Of æons gone away in silence vast
That laughing shall not know, for moments such
Come once, but linger often, and are known
For ever in a corner we did own.

24/4
 (Bangor)

Power?

To be alone again, to be alone
With all that was and can yet be again
The part of man that yet can walk unknown
Upon the map of ages – to refrain
From making of much noise upon this land
And rest upon a Bosom where the world
Has time to wait a while: here, here to stand
Where angels do naught else, while hence are
hurled
The matters of great weight that are not all
That need for ever be, to stand and wait,
To stand and hope, to stand and dare to call
To order where much order ordered ill
The all for which we came – may I this will?

7/5
(Abbadia)

This I command

And when I gaze again at the Unknown
That 'hind this door holds all the all in view,
When in an hour or two all all alone
I see that sees me well, that nothing new
Did ever ever see, when here again
I wait upon a while and smile as Hell
O'er all the cosmos howls, and when in vain
I peep into Tomorrow, nothing well
On this wide world yet stands, unless it be
The placing of my weary head on this
Faint beating that bade all, the all that we
Were bid to do on earth: I have known bliss
But twice in History, and I discern
That not to love 'tis twice in Hell to burn.

11/5
(Abbadia)

Come, cloister, come

And when upon a while we stand again
Where once we stood before, where once we
heard
The murmur of much time; when we regain
The shore whereon before was heard a word
Caught 'tween the æons' pacing, there where
stood
The hooded trav'ler hid, there where the all
Was known unchanged to be, where ancient good
Did act again again 'neath this old call –
To Solitude, the land of many hours,
Where Time has time to be, where much is seen
In gazing in the dark, where sounds have pow'rs
Unheard where words came oft, then soft we
glean
In list'ning with our all a smaller bliss
That passed Earth by 'mid mirth too great for this.

21/5
(in the train)

79

Εἰς τὴν ἔρημον

(Mk 1,13)

To be alone again, to be alone,
And here alone to own the all that is,
For that 'tis his alone that here has known
The meaning of a sound, and only his,
To hear thus coming near the very all
That in much noise walks on. I shall here pause
And halt the cosmos by a sound so small
That none shall know whence stirred the cosmic cause.
Enough of heavy pacing! I shall be
An ear of List'ning made; I shall this bend
Upon the breasts long stifled that to me
For but a moment come. On earth I'll lend
A hand of soft caressing where men's speed
Left long undone the greatest little deed.

6/6
(St Norbert)

Abandoned

(but not by Tiziana)

What is a friend upon the coldest night? What is
a sign
That softens e'en the sound of hard delight
That some in hurting take? What heat benign
Resides in yet a breast not gone away
But there, nay, ever there? What is a friend
If not a healing in a well-known ray
That through the darkness comes the night to
mend?
For in a fondled smile the pharmacy
Of heavy human kind knows more of man
Than sharpest cervic skill, and when I see
A face that would me hold as never can
The clutches of high mirth, I stand alone
And yet not quite alone, not quite alone.

15/6
(Sacred Heart)

Pane, croce e sacramento
troverai sempre in convento

Beth ydyw hyn, fy Nuw, beth ydyw hyn,
Sy'n torri ar ddistawrwydd hir y gell?
Ai gwir y medr dyn yr hyn a fyn
Ei wneud, ei ddweud, er gwaethaf neu er gwell?
Ai dim ond inc a drefna dynged Dyn,
A hyn dan grebwyll un neu ddau a ddaeth
Ar lwybr oes? A oes gan un, ond un,
Hawl grym awdurdod dros ganrifoedd maith?
A phan na fyddom mwy ar erwau mân
Y byw a waeddodd dro, a ddaw yn ôl
Lais adlais un a lefai, neu ryw gân
A fynnai eto ddod? Ai bod yn ffôl
Yw bod am byth yn un, un unig un
Na fynnai fod yn rhan o arall ddyn?

22/6
Pane, croce...:
geiriau'r Abad, gyda gwahoddiad
i wneud cerdd o'r dyfyniad.

Madness and Hell fire

Upon a will awhile hangs all the earth,
But 'tis mine too to utter what may hold
The all at bay. Nay, madness may have worth
Of strangest sanity, and Naught made bold
May will the æons' march if giv'n a pen
And yet an open ear, a heart that sees
'Tween aching lines hid meanings that all men
Are not aye giv'n to see. Nay, loud decrees
Not all the ages govern; there are sounds
Made but of wantings strong that can endure
A storm or two of paper and, 'cross bounds
Of Interdiction heavy, stand secure
Upon a little holding of the world
By one small will, while all to Hell is hurled.

22/6

Er hat uns selig gemacht
und berufen mit einem heiligen Ruf

(2 Tm 1, 9)

When in a bone is seen the all that was
The sound of human kind, when all is done
And earth weighs well the worth of all that has
A moment of high glory, when are won
Upon a last breath heaved the heavy hours
Of everlasting pain or ecstasy,
And when for aye the sway of unknown pow'rs
Is all that these void sockets ever see,
Then, then alone is known what matter here
Did matter unto one that came this way,
And in this long sealed skelet I can hear
A language 'tween clenched teeth that aye and aye
Doth mutter of a moment that came by
For better or for worse where none can die.

24/6
(after opening ven. Abbot's tomb)

Healing

(in a bishop's letter)

To look upon an envelope and see
Sealed yet the morrow waiting to be known,
To hear the stifled word Eternity

Will aye and aye perceive, to sit alone
And open Destiny, to feel the pain
That might enfolded lie, to read and read
And find a heart alive, and to remain
Not sawn asunder yet by sounds that bleed,
But wanted yet on earth, but worth a while
Of list'ning made of pow'r, of hours bid be
What they were called to be: 'tis soft to smile
Hard at a raging æon – History
In black strokes embryonic on one page
Hath stood, stands, here shall stand from age to age.

27/6

Agility, as fast as thought

I have a treasure hid that none on earth
Hath ever seen or known – I enter in
Where man ne'er walked or fumbled, and know mirth
Not heard of human kind: 'hind railings thin
There moves a breast that touches in the night
Not by the moon's known fondlings, not where flesh
Its heat swells high, but nigh a stranger light
At whose fair glow pure soul can soul enmesh.
And I hold all that need be held by touch
There where nought ever touches, I feel here
Thou where thou art, seen Sister, what ne'er clutch
Could hold or press so hard; nay, nearer, near,
Too near I feel thee come where membrane nought
Apart holds soul from soul at angel sport.

28/6
(An enclosed nun, in prayer)

Rumblings

(under the Vatican)

There travels in the air a mighty noise
Of missives made of syllables that fire
The dormant cells of matter grey in poise
'Tween apathy well fed and passion high'r
Than some did deign to think: we winked at all
The fumblings high liturgic that all Hell
'Mid limelight bright and brighter did install
By dint of meaning better than was well.
We bombed the heavy centuries at will
And built square scaffolds theoretic, high,
But there are whiles that would at whiles be still
And for naught but a grain of incense sigh,
For there are times when time trims not its God,
And gazings where e'en Chronos stands unshod.

28/6

Unsaid

A virgin is a land where human hand
Ne'er felt its way, and daylight hours ne'er slept
In rest twice-o'er awaited – 'tis a land
Where stranger never moved, where vigil kept
Held all at gaze well sheathed, where not a part
To eyes unknown belonged, where comings nigh,
Beginnings to exist, sweet pains that smart
Came not to ruffle e'er what gave no sigh.
But virgin unto virgin called to come
A hugeness of two hollows blows to one,
One meeting made of parting, yet where home
In ancient warmness lies – hid, wimpled nun,
Sealed, railed, well nailed: some sighs ne'er heard
Profaned ne'er were by grammar of known word.

29/6

The bleeding, burning Host

(of Venezuala)

To rest upon a breast, to rest on Thee,
My Lord, my God, the all whence but a part
Can be the all to man; to gaze and see
Not what calls home from heart to wanting heart,
But flames unknown – not epidermal hope
Made of thrilled, filled sense tactic, called to be
The centre of two drawings, there where grope
For fulness halves that touch, but Ecstasy:
This is to call upon the universe
And bid an æon halt – this is to touch
The part to move the whole, not to reverse
A Vestal virgin flame from burning such
As Thou wouldst will, but to still one last claim
Upon a will that answers to a name.

3/7
(St Thomas, after singing conventual Mass)

Before an unopened letter

Before my eyes there lies a voice unheard,
A face that ne'er again I shall here see,
A heart that in the night sends out a word,
A being that was not that yet would be.
I shall bid poise a syllable of mirth
That can 'mid air vibrate, or halt a pain –
A pain of wanting more upon this earth
Than might be well, lest Hell a measure gain –
And then I shall in ecstasy full lie
To see the form a line or two may take,
And I shall hold, beholding with the eye,
A soul of Meaning made, that bade me break
The seal of weal long yearned, ere burned be this
Last ember of a stolen folded bliss.

4/7

A new pen

(gift of a friend for Ordination anniversary)

A page has not a voice until a line
Holds in a stroke a molecule or two
That can an æon travel: globules fine
A tingle on a retina, run through
By throbbings of old time, can times bespark,
And there is pow'r upon an hour that comes
To come again, for oft a little mark
Upon a silent page for ever hums.
And when, my sister, thou didst bid me burn
The trace of this thy face for evermore,
Thou didst bestill a ray that here shall learn
Its gentle sound once found ne'ermore to pour
Upon the brain that 'neath the morrow's dawn
Might p'haps have caught an inkling by ink borne.

5/7

Cistercian Compline

(in Latin)

There are some sounds wherein are found again
A Yesterday that was and is not gone.
There are some chords that cervic cells regain
And do again a work not quite undone.
There are some currents in the Lombard air
That ages technic halt – there is a chant
That I have heard before, in moments where
The heart yet green for utterness would pant.
And though there be much loving in the soul,
I will go home and bid this Yesterday,
The one I ever knew, the Morrow whole
Into its image take. This night, I say,
I have heard what shall be, I have heard all:
A *Salve* of old joy doth homeward call.

6/7

Ubera consolationis

(Is 66, 11)

It is not meet to meet upon a land
That Thou, my Lord, wouldst tread and walk
alone.
It is not right to enter here and stand
Where One alone would be, that all would own.
It is not fitting that a human eye
Should gaze at sacrifice not yet consumed,
And 'tis not well that Hell should here brush by
And spark an unmarked virgin calmed and
groomed.
And Yet I know that to mean much to one
Unseen, unknown on earth, to have a place,
A part upon a soul, 'tis 'neath the sun
To have a right to be. 'Tis but a face
That from afar looks on that sees the world
That mattered naught, and unto naught was
hurled.

8/7

Noise

There are too many words upon the air
That carries currents all – the smallest sound
Disfigures meanings great, and only where
Is little said is depth of hearing found.
I have known moments where a silence great
Heard many things, for where clings soul to soul
The matter that here matters carries weight
When in a word unsaid was heard the whole.
And I have heard a sermon of much length
That heard was not for that it would not end,
When but a phrase ends not, for that its strength
It knows unto its echo yet to lend.
For echoes are but spectres, yet live on
There where loud emptied skulls their all have done.

13/7

Oft a Pyrrhic victory

And when upon an æon yet unborn
We lie in sleep unruffled, what of this
Our muttering much done will there be borne
Across the yawning skies? And when long bliss
Or longer damnèd woe is all e'ermore
The knowing that knows all, what then will hours
Of heavy talk upon th'ethereal shore
Of heavier Truth discuss ' mid cosmic pow'rs?
And when, my friend, we matter not as much
As moments once had thought, what little thing
Will hold the weight of endings? Vict'ries such
As mar angelic wings, shall they then ring
Th'alarum of a never ending knell,
Where truth defended prised high gates of Hell?

14/7

Providence

(Gn 50, 20)

There is a Vision in the universe,
And gazing old that waited long for us
To come this way: for better and for worse
We clap a moment's bliss and travel thus
From pain to pain to gain an hour e'er gone,
And on high calcule plot the morrow's course
And shape and preen its visage, and press on
To bid it faster come, without remorse.
But there are moments never meant to be,
And hours that need not happen: there is time
To hold an æon ere it land, to see
If this be all that shall at earth's last chime
Have ever ever been – for seen, long seen,
Was what would be, and what p'haps might have
been.

15/7

Dove si è attesi
il giunger è sempre lieti

To be but wanted is to be but well;
To know that to be known is but a joy
Is to walk well on earth: when one small bell
Awaited rings with joy – while some annoy
With oft unsoftened soundings of the same –
And when a voice long distant comes again
Across an exile sky, when but a name
Called by a bosom warm calms gathered pain:
Then there is in Encounter contact high
Not made of limbs soft touching but hid parts
Of soul and heart commingled, drawing nigh,
Nigh, nearer still, too near for little hearts
Not made for forces such, for touch knows not
A hold of old, old bliss two ne'er forgot.

16/7

The art of the muses

There is a med'cine in the universe
That hovers in the air, as in the page
Wherein it dormant lies, for hours rehearse
The language of a beauty age to age
From brain to brain hands on, and Yesterday
In many morrows lives, for joy once known
May tingle yet a distant unborn day,
And much is heard in touches shared alone.
For Harmony is wholeness twice bid be,
And loudness knows no cry as long as this
Faint echo of true Song, for Melody
Is Truth unuttered well, and sounds of bliss
Have pow'r in regions dark, where marked yet lies
A vibrancy that walked across the skies.

18/7
(after hearing the Abbot Primate)

All our yesterdays

To read again the moments that went by
And hear again a long forgotten sound,
A voice that comes no more across the sky
Where other forces move, to find unbound
Lost rayons once too strong, to hear a song
Once sung by two too close – nay, nay, to smell
An odour that once dazed, to linger long
Where shortness was the all of Heav'n and Hell:
'Tis, sister hid, unseen, that dost not smart,
To hold thee well where holding is no more,
For I perceive that loving has an art
That all the world knew not – what fouled before
By heaviness too high was oft by man
Shall by a virgin stand in wimpled land.

19/7

Icon

O Goodness that made all, I hear Thee call
And, kneeling, know what I must be on earth.
It is not to much freezing of the all
That in the breast yet stirs, but unto mirth
Conferred and heard and touched and handed on
That Thou wouldst move my days – it is to this
Soft kindling of a joy where naught e'er shone,
And shedding but at whiles a little bliss.
For I have pow'r to heal and pow'r to harm,
And some have wants I know and thoughts I hear,
But I shall leave much warmth and none alarm
In coming close where none hereto drew near.
To love I shall be bold, I shall hold all
In but a little daring e'er so small.

21/7

Acme

(1 Cor 7, 36)

There is a beauty yet in age unused
And virgin years live where ne'er a man
Did trample or ill tread, and where abused
Was not a heart that wanting, waking can
To much in losing stir, serenity
And calm of dormant dreams ne'er called to be
Can leave a once fair forehead merrily
The same in simple impish rovings free.
And when upon an æon none e'ermore
Shall gaze upon a wimpled face I know,
Will pain again be known where pain before
In thee, lost face, long shone – will years bestow
A thought for thought unheard, where many miles
Two pairs of eyes held aye from piercing smiles?

20/7

Lætabuntur in cubilibus suis

(Ps 149, 5)

O little child, so wild upon the night,
Canst thou not rest upon a blessing found.
Let me but hide within this bosom white
Not in high vision gazing, not high bound,
But as a child secure, in purest rest
Upon his mother's soul, where all the world
Is safe and kept afar – Oh! blessed nest,
Protect this little bundle in thee curled,
For I seek not thy body but thy soul,
That though incarnate meets upon the night
Another that it knows, for oft the whole
Is had where nought is sought, while to ignite
Much wanting is to wait on flames too strong,
For 'tis but rest that can yet linger long.

22/7
(St Mary Magdalen)

Prodigy

This miracle I see from day to day
Behind a candle shining, this fair sun
That came from the beyond and cast away
The doubt that once did gather, and undone
Left all the whiles of Satan, this our light,
My gentle, faithful sister, calls me home,
And in an exile's land, in this long night,
I hear again a voice that bids me come.
For we belong to that of which we are,
And acres have hid roots that yet can pull
From shore to distant shore, and from afar
Blue eyes I once loved well, pure hearts yet full
Of little joys unfouled yet calmly smile
That knew that I'd resist but for a while.

26/7

’Αγάπη

(1 Tm 1, 5)

There are huge tears in corners of the earth,
And hearts that thought of love here oft have found
Refined and finest hurt where once a mirth
In little breasts had stirred, once heard the sound
Of kindly words that then were thought to be
The all of all – and smallest signs did mean
The fulness of all sense when History
Did hang upon a moment two had seen.
O chastity of soul! The whole is played
Upon this fondling no more in the dark
Within a world unwed. O! gentle maid,
Return to thy one Lord, whose sacred mark
Upon a day we shared on thee was laid.
Thy soul I may love well, but only this
May I upon a lonesome night e'er kiss.

27/7

104

Tra cent'anni non ci sarò più

And when upon an æon we no more
These tickings thin yet tread, when in the air
No echo of our splashings on this shore
Of seconds come and gone one ruffle there
Again leaves evermore, when not a word
From long resounding larynx comes again,
What then, my friend, of this our hour yet heard
Will th' unborn morrow's ear that day regain?
Will there be room for little little things
In this old Cosmos vast that lingers on?
Will frail a beauty that a music sings
In decomposing leave its work undone?
And when we are no more, sweet breast, will this
Strange melody we heard know aught of bliss?

27/7

In der Liebe eingewurzelt und gegründet

(Eph 3, 17)

It is but love that makes the heart of man
What it should be, what it can be, what all
Would have it ever be, for loving can
Of cosmic truth know more in touchings small
Than ecstasy grown wild, and mildness holds
More happiness than Sense, for hence we move
From souls that touch where ne'er a clutch enfolds
To lands of utterness where angels love.
For at this Altar, King, I sing of home,
And hold what holds me well, what holds all Hell
And Heav'n in its old palm, and calm I come
To where all loves repose, for in this bell
That signs Thy treading here, I hear Thee say
'Twas for this love that all love else made way.

11/8
 (St Clare)

Many confessions

(in the confessional made in 1696)

O! healing in a box where knocks all Hell
To have a place 'hind faces never seen!
O! ancient wood, where stood 'neath this old smell
The æons held in poise, where flames had been...
O! tears bid spring again, O! pain oft heard
To be in this sound lifted – here moves all
That matters for all time: a little word
Adjusts Eternity in whispers small.
O! damnèd world, move on and pass calm by
This cupboard of sealed woe, and go away
To height of bliss where peeps an ancient sky
Bid bend no more as once of yesterday
That tingles of old sin knew well, knew well,
But took a while to smile at raging Hell.

12/8

Yr hen gyffesgell

Y mae i bren hen wên, hen wefr a ddaw
Yn ôl, yn ôl o hen eonau Dyn,
Ac yma clywaf adlais pell na thaw,
A gwyrth yn hen eiriynnau eto lŷn.
Y mae fan hyn gyfarfod rhwng dau fyd
A hen iachâd a wybu echdoe lu.
Y mae i ddeigryn lais huodledd mud
A ddywaid eto lawer am a fu.
Y mae byddaru lle mae sibrwd main
A rwyg agendor Nef: y cyffwrdd hwn
Heb wyneb a heb gorff, awdurdod sain
I uffern yrr yr eithaf, drymaf pwn,
Ac yma saif, yn arwydd croes, yr oll
A ffoes o hen, hen afael Cythraul coll.

13/8

Offeren cefn gwlad

Y mae i le fodfeddi nad ŷnt mwy
Yn rhan o erwau byd, o diroedd Dyn,
A chonglau yma sydd ac iddynt hwy
Gudd rymusterau oesoedd hen a lŷn.
Y mae fan hyn ar farmor allor wen
Gyffyrddiad a fu gynt, angylaidd su,
Hen siffrwd traed, ac yma 'hwnt i'r llen
A'th guddia Di, daw sain adenydd lu.
Cans er ond un a saif yn wyneb hon
O anferth henaidd Ras, nid un yw côr
Yr anwel seraff dân ddaw'n don ar don
O driphlyg sanctaidd gân ar wydraidd fôr
Lle bu i eraill ddod, i eraill fod
Yn cyffwrdd am eiliedyn wreiddiau Bod.

22/8

109

Profound call

(on small telephone, between two cloisters)

O! little thing, so huge upon the air
That holds the world at bay – I hear thee say
More in the softest sound where none walks there
Than in the pacing voices of a day.
For words too oft o'erheard last seldom long,
And many sounds outpoured return as light
In what they bear as they 'neath weightless
throng
Of messages hard brought in thoughtless might.
O virgin pure, of surer peace made whole,
In silence of high pow'r call me yet home
To regions that I know, where soul and soul
'Cross oceans vast at last can boldly come
To matter chattered well, to this old land
Where none of noise defiled may vilely stand.

24/8

Warmth

I have a call, and 'tis a simple thing,
Oft heard without a word, without a noise,
And I know well what messages here bring
The silent hours where all stands yet in poise.
I have a call so small that all the earth
Shall pass it by, for nought to limelight brought
Will bid it shine, yet souls of little worth
At whiles can mean a smile by some yet sought.
I have a call, and this is all I know
'Mid rubrics high that sanctify much pain:
'Tis but to be, 'tis but to bid bestow
From soul to soul an essence very plain.
Good Lord, 'tis simple, this my little call.
I shall pass by, and do a thing so small...

26/8

Vox Christi

(through a gadget)

A sound from Erin stirs and bids me come
Across the skies to distant westward climes
To stillness heard before, to signs of home,
To minutes shoved no more by changèd times,
To eyes well known, as pure as ancient skies
Pierced oft by softest pleading where arose
The agèd Celtic litanies, the cries
Long silenced by the wind that onward blows.
I will come home, my friend, and to the end
An old flame not quenched quite yet strike again.
A goodness in this land this noon doth send
In cellular soft magic writing plain
Of light upon a night where damnèd Hell
Would have me with Confusion ever dwell.

28/8

112

Moment of truth

A day has dawned before that dawns again,
And these soft rays that warm yet call me home.
A week or two shall come ere I regain
A desert isle I know where once did roam
The feet of youth, 'neath truth of plainness seen
Where Thou, my Lord, didst speak, where Thou didst say,
"Come, come; come closer now, stand where have been
The feet of ones made whole: here stand and stay."
O peace of soul! The wholeness of the all
In Solitude refound! The bounds of prayer
Contaminated ne'er by tingles small
Of currents calling hence! Nay, nay, but there
A Presence in the midst, Thou didst bid do
Full naught, but only be; be naught but true.

8/9

A blessing and a touch

(for Marcellina)

There are worlds hid beneath a little breast,
Strange things that eye sees not, that not a word
Reveals, but yet, sweet maid each morn here blest,
I hear thee well, for oft far more is heard
In molecules that touch than in much noise
That pounds too oft upon a softer sound
Wherein much meaning lies. A second's poise
Holds cheek to virgin cheek when homeward bound.
Farewell, hid gem. But wilt thou come again
Morn after morn where blessing no more comes
Upon a brow in prayer? Will there be pain
Where warmth came but a while? Long age benumbs
A blessing that singed all. Goodbye, my friend.
Beginnings ne'er should be that soon must end.

8/9

Go back, sons of men

(Ps 89 [90], 3)

Go back, good soul, to th'arms that bid thee be,
And travel o'er the ancient æons home
Along a journey that long history
Has age to age revealed. The hour has come
To come and go no more, and, 'hind this door
That soon must close thy world, there stands and
waits
A cosmos that shall stand and wait e'ermore
Where stand and wait in vain the ill-spun fates.
We thee with unction send upon thy way
And cheek to cheek thee greet, yet this strange
road
That thou anon shalt see, in our dark day
May not thee plot or mark, nor yet forebode
What welcome thee awaits. One chance was
giv'n.
A little tick ticks on in Hell and Heav'n.

9/9
(after anointing)

Serenity

A time will be when time will be no more
By these fond faces fondled, when no smile
Of goodness known awhile will winter thaw
Upon the Celtic shore, when Latin guile
Will by dint of suggesting woo not home
To sharing of old warmth, 'tween breasts where
heat
Ne'er knew its bliss to hide, when ne'er shall come
To shed a ray of blessing faithful feet.
Goodbye, strange land, that handed on my God
In christic hands on fire; goodbye, wild youth
Of human kind aglow: the gentler sod
Of Erin bids rest on a softer truth.
For Sense is not the all of ecstasy,
And eyes sealed evermore may better see.

14/9

116

Heaped skeletons

(from the bubonic plague)

And when upon an æon we lie still
Next to our skelet friends who grin for e'er
Into th'unhurried void, when will and will
Strive no more 'neath the troubled breast, there where
The cosmos lay in poise, when noise no more
From lips for ever silent comes forth hence
To change the course of skulls as once before
It oft unbid could do – when naught comes thence:
What then will these strange sockets ever see
'Hind long horizons that full eyes see not?
And then, my friend, what endless end shall we
Make of our small beginning – when forgot
Are tingles that were ours, what hours aye, aye
Shall linger on for ever and a day?

19/9
(during the excavations)

117

Visage di bonté

(Dom Chautard à la fin de sa vie)

May this be said one day, may this be said:
"There was but goodness in this part of earth."
When o'er a passing breath a soft tear shed
Recalls a little giggle of sweet mirth
That shall not come again, let this be heard
Above the din of passing, that once here
A fondle lost was known, where but a word
Brought planets of stray soul a little near.
Let there be pain to know that grains of bliss
In this small angle of the cosmic void
May come again no more – let only this
Be left where naught is left where once there toyed
With forces not of man the shades that were
Giv'n on this stage a little while to stir.

19/9

Finalmente ho trovato una persona
chi mi pensa

What 'tis to be a thought in but a brain,
Knows only who shone not, who was not fair
To gazing eyes, that gazed not at the pain
Beneath the uncared bosom that was there,
The object of no want, for cast away
Was one not giv'n to run the gallant pace,
And no heat rose and fell upon a day
For one with beauty marred in scarred a face.
Yet beauty comes again where fairness bright
On many gazings shed too oft is known,
And, little child, this mildness of thy light
Draws more my eyes than fairness overshown.
There are some parts too secret to be shared,
And beauty full and sacred was not bared.

20/9
Finalmente...: Message from handicapped Anna Rita.

Desire

O little child, wouldst thou too come this way
To th'ancient Isle, and for a while know peace
Known once upon an æon, in a day
When time had time to be – to th'Isle where cease
The noises that noise all, the sounds that press
To move too quickly o'er this little course
That carries all along, where merriness
Is made of Soul high wired to damnèd Force?
Come, come, my Sister; come to gentler joys
Where 'neath a song and blessing days are known
That we have known before where we no noise
Before the Master made, where we were shown
How little Joy doth need, where no desire
Clouds th'all that is, enough, all, all entire.

25/9

Utter silence

O! night of peace, in Erin's sacred isle
That waited for a while, unhurried yet
To be as all the earth – O! tender smile
Of faces long, long known! O! joy where met
Lives kept apart by years where much has been
That need no more be known, for here at last
A sound once known is heard, a land is seen
Where one awhile may shelter from the blast.
I have come home, and here henceforth shall be
In simple blessings spent, in moments shed
That Thou alone shalt own: at last I see
The land whereon I'll rest and lay my head.
For on this night I light a little light
Long known, long known, and not forgotten quite.

6/10
(St Bruno)

Calculating deaths

The tapping of a moment lingers long
For one that comes no more upon this way,
And oft a flash did dash the softest song
That nevermore shall rock the close of day.
The seconds that tick on tick no more on
There where they may not come, and we know not
The vision of the eye whose work is done,
That sees naught and sees all – e'er, where none rot.
We cease to be not quickly as we come
Upon a night to shine, and ecstasy
That was our first beginning our long home
May not perforce make gay – nay, we shall see
In tapping of all time, what rhymes best e'er
With what our ticking seconds chisel there.

23/10
(in solitude)

On April the eighth, 1984, the Holy Father explained, on the
occasion of the military Jubilee (cf. *Osservatore Romano*,
French edition, no. 16, 1984): "Since approximately 145,000
people die every day over the earthly globe, one can say that
people die at every moment." Over a period of twenty-five years,
since population has notably increased, the number of daily
deaths has undoubtedly likewise increased. It would hence seem
that the approximation of two deaths per second is at the present
period in human history very plausible. If 2 people die every
second, in 1 minute, 60 x 1 (= 120) die. In 1 hour, 60 x 120 (=
7,200) die . In 1 day, 24 x 7,200 (= 172,800) die.

Oh... Casa!... Ti amo, mio fratello

There are some words that come across the air
By means of means new fangled, there are signs
That calmly blast the innards that here share
The thought of thought twice thought and
brought by lines
And dint of magic high from sky to land
Of innocence and bliss where troubled not
Were depths of man laid still, till in my hand
A little screen beams pulses long forgot.
O child so wild with playing, what strange game
Doth Grace thus bid thee play? Did this day come
At which I see a virgin with no shame
To use a word, nay, words, that call on home?
Come, little child, if this be thy fair will,
And warm thy soul in safe a Celtic chill.

24/10

Lost

O priest of God, the least of men on earth
Has hope more great, more bright than this thy night
That evermore shall be, for hours of mirth
At whiles consoled thy nest, but thy blest sight
Could not in peace behold what thou didst hold
The morrow as it came with sorrow high
High, high at th'Altar's height, where thou wast bold
To consecrate the sacred hotly nigh.
O dimming of a light! What might is here
To tempt in envy's heat, from hatred pure,
The flock yet left on earth, and hellward steer
By dint of angel hint, new fiends to lure
With Luciferic glee, for that no hope
A doubly damnèd soul bid upward grope?

26/7

First Mass

(under new modalities)

Ten years have passed since first I held Thee high,
High, higher yet upon the cosmos all
That in thy hand did stand, for Godhead nigh
Did come upon the humming of a call
That æons split, and hit Satanic Hell
That would not have this be: I see again
Thee stand in this my hand and hold Thee well
O'er Erin's land, where this time I'll remain.
I have come home, and roaming far and wide
Shall be no more. Before me I can see
An Eden known of old, and horrified
A legion of bold fiends. "This shall not be,"
Seethed Hell in foulèd frenzy, yet it stands,
And dusk this night doth bury distant lands.

1/11

(All Saints)

First sight of home

There is a Vision that thought long on this,
A Kindness in the air that knows me well.
There is in coming home a little bliss
That chuckles at the rage of damnèd Hell.
There is in stillness found a sound of Peace
That echoes ancient days, and ways oft lost
Are by a patient Brain e'ermore bid cease
Their wand'rings long to wend 'mid Chaos tossed.
O Master, here we meet where Thou didst wait
Upon an æon leaning; there is space
'Tween wall and little wall a nonsense great
In madness glad to weave. For to enlace
The Godhead all in gazing is a crime
That shall demand the flinging of all time.

2/11
(All Souls)

Ellen

Goodbye, God bless, sweet sister of an hour
And hours of long ago that did return
And through thee live again. Ah! what strange pow'r
Doth womankind yet hold the earth to turn
Upon an axis wild, where mildest sound
suffice to move high mitres, where but sense
And goodness Celtic pure steel canons pounds
In fields of caustic learning laden dense.
'Tis well while Hell raves on and damns the skies
To own a chuckle yet – upon a land
That knew in ancient madness what was wise
And dared to beckon by a woman's hand.
Kind Ellen, epics rage and empires go,
But stratagem ne'er was as though dost know.

4/11

It seems unreal

What 'tis to rest upon the breast of God
When all the world doth rage, what 'tis to find
Beneath a cosmos rocking one small sod
Untrodden by hard haste, and leave behind
Loud mutterings that matter little more
There where but Godhead speaks – to be, to be
And do but little else: 'tis to hear roar
The winds of passing Time o'er History.
I shall stand still, nay, kneel for hours untold
Until they come no more, until naught comes
But hours unknown, unmade. I shall make bold
To waste the all of living, for there hums
O'er this void quire oft an angel wing
That patters and bid better, better sing.

5/11

Writing on the wall

O double signature left by a God
Upon a hermit's wall! O call made known
Twice o'er across the æons that did plod
In aimless amble on! O glimmer shown
To be in all that glistered that one true
That beamèd but for me – Ah! thing of things
That in the cosmic engine did break through
The sound of broken fixings where all clings:
O Providence, Thou hast an ink, a quill
Called Happ'nings, and a writ of script not seen
But heard, and only heard, heard but when still
And list'ning well... Lord, I before have been
In this old place called Peace. I have Thee heard,
But now th'oft thought soft spies one uttered word.

8/9

Bishop at the door

Come in, my lord, and see what but a word
Of thine can do on earth: a little ink,
A mitred message by electrons heard,
Can by a Brain well drilled be but the link
To make a matter happen there where thought
On heavy void did feed. Ah! this sweet name
Now writ upon a door the realms of Nought
Did paint for years fantastic... Nothing came –
Till thou, kind head, didst listen to the heart
And read more 'tween two scribblings than long hours
Of list'ning without ears did learn in th'art
Of tapping embryonics and hid pow'rs.
God bless thee, little man; may Erin live
Upon a blasting blessing one did give.

12-13/11

Der Herr ist in seinem heiligen Tempel

(Ps 11 [10], 4)

I light a lamp this day that will burn on
While earth sleeps onward t'ward the darkest night
That Erin ever saw, and Grace that shone
n souls that travelled 'neath an ancient light
I shall here keep afresh, for healing deep
Comes 'neath the wings this Sun that shall rise
On this small part of earth, where angels peep
Within behind this door that hides the skies.
Come, Lord; come, Lord of hosts; come, King of kings,
And stand within this temple spread for Thee.
Together we shall be, where little wings
Soft flutter where we utter History.
For matters great are done by Matter small,
And doing naught to death, I have done all.

27/11
(after placing Bd Sacrament in tabernacle)

Dyma babell

Mae yma fan i Dduwdod, man i Ddyn,
Man i angylion cudd, cans lle y mae
Eu Teyrn, ei osgordd hefyd ddaw, ac Un
Nid unig yw'n ei gell: i'r pur, hoff bai
Yw'r ongl fach lle rhoddodd Ef ei draed,
Ac wrth oleuo'r llusern hon mi wn
Am Oen a'm carodd i, mi wn am Waed
Iachâd a rydd i'r prudd dan drymaidd bwn.
A hon fydd fangre lle cyferfydd hoen
Ag ing colledig rai: y mae fan hyn
Ryw wên a'u hedwyn hwy – dyrchefir Oen
Dros allor a thros ynys: Duwdod gwyn
A ddaliaf yn fy llaw nes daw y dydd
Na fydd na drws na rhith i'w gadw'n gudd.

27/11
(o flaen y tabernacl newydd)

Thebaid revisited

O sound of peace beneath the patting rain
That centuries have known! O land where all
Stands strangely still – I hear, I hear again
What never has gone by. The ages call
E'en from the stones before me, where the quire
Its voice here no more finds: this little place
Is where I shall Thee find; and Patrick's fire
To Cianan handed on, did this spot trace.
My Lord, here present 'mid an angel throng,
I shall here cease to do what can yet wait
Another busy man, for time for Song
Unhurried and unjarred shields 'hind this gate
That separates a little, little land
Wherein a moment caught had time to stand.

30/11

Thebaid...: The Thebaid reappeared in Ireland, affirmed
Montalembert, in *Monks of the West* (quoted by A. Cogan in
The Diocese of Meath, Ancient and Modern).

To Cianan handed on...: St Patrick formed St Cianan and set him
over the first see set up by him here in the country.

This spot...: Duleek Abbey stands before the window. *Damhliag*
(Duleek) signifies a stone church, and would have been the central
point of the monastic establishment.

Angelus Domini descendit de cælo

There are before me presences – a throng,
A legion I see not, for Thou alone
At heart of winter night does comp'ny own
Not as at these dark hours, 'neath eyelids sealed
And members held, is known and known again
As e'er by sons of men, but in a field
Of ether high, where ties of old remain.
For I hear voices in these silent stones
That Cianan set and others chiselled well,
And all, all, all alone I hear these tones
Of psalmic prayer hit hard on jaws of Hell
That bid this come no more, that bid this be
The end of endless wasted History.

2/12

A home that did not come

Beginnings have an ending upon earth,
And morrows once unknown their sorrows bear.
O pious Union, move into the mirth
Of common day, clad 'mid the fullest glare
Of old Prémontré's splendour, and come home
To where thou dost belong, but leave behind
A child that loved thee well, who may not come
Again to this his cell or home here find.
Move on, my brethren, to an ancient day
In Erin also known, but walk withal
To noisome pestilence, for here the way
Doth part for e'er and aye, and mutters small
Lead here to endless talking, while afar
A home awaits where Haste may days ne'er mar.

27/1/8
(Sant'Antimo)

Irish eyes

("The Lord has given you a nice smile.")

There is a goodness yet upon this land,
Not made of man, not made of human kind,
And there are corners where old moments stand
In poise, where noises new did not yet bind
The all to utter Progress, where a while
A little little while had time to be
All that it need but be, where but a smile
Could yet know how to glow, and merrily.
O little face, that paced not hard in haste
To please but yet the next that never came,
But me alone, for naught, for utter waste
Of energy o'erspent, not e'en thy name
Shall I e'er know, yet know I shall for days
The meaning of a ray that idly strays.

9/4

Pregnant

What'tis to know that one that I knew well
Hath known too much on earth, and that the moon
Did witness once an hour that very Hell
Did ponder long – where Song its heav'nly boon
At that same hour once gave there where now weep
Torn angels and a maid now riv'n in twain –
And bid ayemore another vigil keep
O'er budding life borne in a bliss of pain...
– O little breast, the nest of heavy grace
Unto the winds hot blown where something moved
Too great for thy hid softness, ne'er thy face
Of cherub glow, glow shall where someone loved
Not what was fair within, but parts of thee
That he could not let be, and now are three.

16/4

Angel text

(from an enclosed nun who could not

renew her vows)

Come, cloistered beam, and shine upon this land
Of simple things, where clings an hour or two
Of what need not move on, for here the hand
Of hastened harm and Progress marched not through
The sacred acre giv'n: here Time may be
What it was meant to be, here Song may come
In tones that stones know well that patiently
Awaited their return. Here, here is Home –
My sister, my pure Sister, if He will
That too lay thy anchor while the hours
Know not as once to amble: here yet still
Thy little head shall rest, where old blest Pow'rs
'Cross nocturns long and song unhurried, full
To where we ever were soft homeward pull.

16/4

Futility

(Figlio mio, quando mai gli uomini, così lenti a comprendere, si renderanno conto della futilità di tutte quelle cose per cui sprecano tempo ed energie?)

There are too many efforts on the earth
That better were not made; there is much weight
Into the long void sent; there oft was mirth
Far greater in the simple than the great,
And joy did tingle more for that it came
Than when in calcule high it should have been,
And Wanting was the ruin of the same,
While happy eyes did rest on what was seen.
I am alone upon a little isle
Where tingles come and go, but I have all,
All, all, I say, for I can rest a while
Not saddened by th'unheld, for here the small,
Is hugely large beheld, and I need not
Be damned by bliss aye willed and never got.

14/4
Figlio mio,…: Words of Jesus to Mons.
Ottavio Michelini in 1975

Kind words

What is a sound upon a hurting ear,
A syllable or two that warms the all,
A meaning never thought, a breast brought near
That yesterday beat not – what is a call
Uncalled that broke the night and from a cell
Another cell did wake; what 'tis to know
That for a heart unknown an hour did dwell
A while again where 'twas, where ling'rings glow:
'Tis this to tingle yet 'mid mingled pain
That some thought well to leave, this is to heave
A sigh where once drew nigh what ne'er again
Unto a heart shall come, this is to weave
Of meanings small hid fibres that can be
The matter that can mutter History.

1/5

O! night

I am not here alone, all, all alone,
Nor is the night here long where long was gone
The comfort of its hours, and, where unknown
Th'encounter of much heat, a meeting shone
'Mid flick'ring light, hid from the sight of Earth
That sees but what can please, yet dreamt not all
That could yet tingle where a lesser mirth
Did still a crave yet simple and yet small.
The world is full of hurting, called to be
By wanting much, by panting much for hours
That pain in coming not. Felicity
Was lost for that 'twas sought, while there were pow'rs
Hard by our side that few e'er thought to touch,
For that to hold perforce meant and to clutch.

10/5

Suicide

Come, little child, come from far far away
And lay thy weary soul awhile on me.
An hour within a lap may more allay
Than capsules round that bound Eternity.
Live on, and know a joy that can yet come
For that two eyes yet open with the dawn,
Not on the æons dim far far from home
But on a place of rest for one forlorn.
A nest there is for one that all the world
Passed by in haste; a memory shall call
Long from thy rested head that, blasted, hurled
Thou'dst have for aye and aye in seconds small –
A mem'ry that for thee could not have been,
If little eyes nought 'yond their tears had seen.

10/5

142

Sunday Mass

(at the Hermitage)

And I thought not that, coming home to Thee,
My silent Friend, to end all noise that came,
I would upon thy day not lonely be
And but by angels seen, but that the name
Of incense sweet and Latin old and quaint
Would draw to this hid home a merry band
Of little little souls, that not a taint
Did reach from Teaching's bleached and damaged land.
Come, come, my angels, huddle 'neath your King,
And hear a tongue that well your heart doth know
To be the sound to which more meanings cling
Than oft in pounded verbiage nude did flow.
Come, cherub smiles, and beam awhile herein,
For there is silence in an angel's din.

11/5

143

Destroy the letters

To burn a voice upon a page that lies
Hard by the breast that hears its silent call;
To muffle aye what huffles where it dies
In cinders that hide all; to let here fall
Into oblivion long a song so fair
That none but one that heard it could e'er seize
'Neath shocks borne by a stroke or two drawn there,
That they might hold a boldness that did please –
To sigh upon an ember, 'tis to weep
Upon a breast I know, that none e'er saw,
To pierce high grilles and wimples and to peep
Into a land of warmth that much did thaw,
And to say, "Go, sweet maid, where He bade be
A virgin ever be that none may see."

Little people

(filling the chapel)

What is a child upon the stratosphere,
A little one that wonders yet at Earth
To which it came from nought, unsought – yet near
To whence it came, the same in mirth
As th'angels that came not, yet stand high o'er
Its shifting for a while? What is a smile
Upon a trusting face? Where gazed before
The eyes of new-sparked Soul that dozed awhile?
Come, come to this your King, sweet merry men
And women harmed not yet by foulèd noise,
And on small knees gaze upward as once when
Your soul's green iris in a fraction's poise
Came from that Face that beamed us, that said, "Be
Another twinkle of Eternity."

15/6

In questa casa c'è solo Amore

What 'tis to live alone and not alone,
But only with a heat that bade us be;
What 'tis to own a corner where is known
No presence but a warmth; what 'tis to see
No eyes that utter pain; what 'tis to hear
No sound but voices fond; what 'tis to rest
Unhurried 'tween two hours, and to be near
A heart wherein awhile we made our nest –
'Tis this to own a land where we can die
Not on worn moments marred, where barred was all
That could have been on earth, where mirth did lie
Beyond the clasp that grasped all but the small
And little little thing that bade us sing
Upon a nothing that did something bring.

Lead, kindly light

There are some moments marked with other things
That are not made of earth, whose worth is such
That unto wand'ring seconds something clings
Which all the hours to be can calmly touch.
I have stood there where stood a heart I know
And held that held a hand still loud in poise,
And I heard, holding high and bending low
In gestures old, of all the oldest noise.
For Silence is the language of this place,
And Hurriedness holds still, for there's a while
waste in halted haste beneath this Face,
That thou, my friend, dost see, there where the smile
Is not of but an Angel, but of Him
Whom here, aye here, thou too didst palp all dim.

2/8
(after singing old Mass with Newman's chalice)

Bombshell

(in a message)

Come, little one, and rest thy head awhile
Upon a breast where nestled once thy past.
Thy face that aye since then did coyly smile
From this framed card so hard, did smile its last
O'er years of hurting long; thy song so sweet
Upon the night oft heard, here stirred the cells
Of Mem'ry's heavy sigh; thy cry, thy heat
Of wanting but a peace where goodness dwells –
This did not go away, and here I say
It need not ever go, for I thee know,
My little, little one, and 'tis thy plight
Of wanting to be His that is to show
The way to bid it be, for I see all
Upon the face of texted letters small.

12/8
(after receiving Sr Nicoletta's words)

Le cose desiderate più a lungo
sono le più belle

When in the night we catch a little light
Afar, afar that as a star beams on
A lone and darkling way, when there is might
In but a textèd sound to leave undone
The ravels of much pain, when here again
We grasp a ray of fondliness and say,
 "I shall take all," then there is huge a gain
In risk and danger loud upon a day.
And I perceive that I am not alone
Upon the lonely earth, where mirth is high
In but a little thing, for though I own
No heart but thine, my King, there travel nigh
At whiles high beams of fondness that mean all,
And Bliss is made of rayons hugely small.

26/8

La tua preghiera è forte

And can it be that this hid little place
Shall hold awhile another on the way
To glory from the blast, that yet a face
Of tenderness and mirth shall cast some day
An anchor on this shore, that more shall be
Of our soft unheard singing where no eye
Did gaze at this our dazèd harmony
Made all of ancient sound rebound on high?
O little thing, wilt tuck at last thy wing
And settle on a star, where oddest hours
Can patter thy way Home; wilt come and cling
To sparkles that come forth, and walk 'mid pow'rs
Too great for thee, too great to let thee be
A flotsam missed upon Eternity?

Exorcism

There are deep in the depths some depths so deep
That puzzlement alone remains when they are heard
Upon our stage to rant: we mortals peep
Into a world forgot, whence ne'er a word
Returns to let us know what land was found
By pilgrim and by pilgrim passing on
And on and on where Onwards has no bound,
For ghosts can journey long from works ill-done.
And I thought no that Judas came again
Upon our land to meddle, or that one
Long silent had a voice, wherein from Pain
Untold, the old old Fiend in damnèd fun
Would giggle at the high credulity
Of mitred heads that belched Eternity.

15/9
(Exorcism carried out in Germany, August – September 1975.)
The text of the exorcism is found in an account given by Fr
Bonaventure Meyer in *Marianisches Schriftenwek*, Trimbach, CH-
4632, Switzerland, 1981.

Dear, dear Father Abbot

(Dom Columcille)

There is a goodness in this ancient land
That I know well, and though in accent strange
It reach the alien ear, the gentle hand
And tongue that sends a word, within its range
Of unexpected moving, moves much pain
Beyond baned Mem'ry's sight, for though a page
Be silent in its coming, markings plain
At times mark hugely all, and blasted rage
I see, I see, need ne'er e'er e'er have been
Or wand'rings none did own: I should have known
Before, long, long before, when first was seen
The kindness of these eyes, that Love alone
Is what the cloister means, and 'twas but this
That need have been enough for simple bliss.

17/9

He'll come to you without your calling

The laughter of a little one, a band
Of little, little ones, is language known
To horse and man alike, and safe the hand
That feeds the kindly friend that knows its own
And stoops to half a world – aha! Blest joy
Made all of simple things, where clings old time
To clothes of moded hue – ah! questions coy
That ask for leave to play on land sublime...
But come, of course, sweet voices, fill the air
Where angels, like you, play about their King
Exposed here 'fore your fondlings , for there
where
A goodness comes to stroke, an ancient wing
Holds like to like, and likes to hear the sound
Of friends yet dumb that some old language
found.

17/9

Alas

I hear upon the silence one great word
That stills all others, drives all others hence
And bids me say no more; this night I heard
Upon the darkest night a calling whence
All callings e'er to be in me shall find
A place to be, a place to rest, to lie
Upon a bosom opened; nay, the blind
And noisome gazing ne'er the eye
That for a silence waited e'er perceived,
And more with eyelids fastened oft was seen
Than by orifices wide that heaved
And spluttered all where small sound would have
been
A little more aware of little things,
For much upon a softness often clings.

19/9

Voglio stare dove sta Lei

O little child, let me thee hold again
Upon the night that knows the sight of love
Not made of touch but of such wanted pain
Of being one in thought where nought doth move
But hurting bliss, the kiss of soul on soul
That rested in a heat where all did meet
Of knowing and of having, for the whole
At whiles is less than th'earnest when complete.
O! happiness of holding but a heart
That rest could find in but a knowing well
That from the world two might yet come apart
And hold enough to hold the nether Hell
At bay, agog, agog that two should dare
To love awhile and smile while demons glare.

23/9

The jumping church

This is a land where strange, strange things combine
Their ways, where days that were live on
Upon the morrow's walls, where calls of Thine
Leave not in peace a work too quickly done
And bid us not think lightly on a stone
Hewn once to hold a God, where plod would yet
A soul not blest or shriv'n, that could not own
A place on earth or sky – nay, we forget
That moments linger long 'yond this long wall
That severs time asunder: blunders here
Cost æons of old hurt, that aye shall call
From age to dawning age, where little fear
Is known where known is little of the blaze
Swift kindled, yet ne'er dwindled in its daze.

28/9

Mass in the country

(Bellewstown)

There is a joy upon a simple thing
And beauty yet on earth in little sounds,
Where in a cosmic heave a world can cling
To corners where a yestersound redounds.
There is a place where faces yet are glad
To see a ray of darkness where the roar
Of netherdungeons grows in howls too mad
For Sense, had sense not sensed it once before.
There is a knowing on an ancient land
Not made of claps and trinkets but of all
That in a word moves yet, for here I stand
Upon a lazy æon where doth call
The truth of yesterday and yesterday
That somehow came and hurried not away.

5/10

A year

There is a silence in the air, that knows
Whence it has come; there is a place where moves
The passing of all days: four walls where flows
The trickling of old tears, where hidden loves
'Tween breasts and Breasts divine may nestle well
And be allowed to be, to see where all
May wait awhile while greater things yet yell
To be the all of all that can enthral.
For I thought not, on writing but a word
To one on high, that nigh, so nigh, could be
The meeting of two worlds, or that reheard
Would be again the plainness that to me
Meant home, when roaming on henceforth may cease,
For in His perfect Will is found our peace.

6/10
(St Bruno)

A hug is the shortest distance
between friends

What 'tis to hold a and hold a little child
That nestles in a rest of soft pressed arms;
What 'tis to fondle well the bundle mild
Whose wildness oft a softer wildness calms;
What 'tis to circle all the wide wide world
Of but a little man; what 'tis to know
That soul can hold a soul ere it be hurled
Upon a journey long where problems grow:
'Tis to behold with eyelids tightly sealed
The fairness of the all, for members small
Bespeak the Arms that made us, and revealed
Was more by silence than by oft a call
To heat of bliss swift mangled by its pull
To fullness of high pressing hard and dull.

16/10

Grinding of teeth

(Mt 25, 30)

When I think on upon what on and on
And on and on shall go with ne'er a pause;
When I behold the pow'r of one day done,
The fact of once an act, th'effect a cause
Can have upon an æon that shall not
Conclude its long beginning; when awhile
I get a thought where wrought and aye forgot
Was some sweet mirth that on the earth did smile:
Then here, safe 'fore this flame, I breathe a sigh
Of sorrow for a morrow that comes ne'er
Upon the night of sinning that was high
In bliss ere its long kiss, its gazing bare
Its eyelids ope'd again where pain alone
Alone, alone in demon hiss is known

17/10

Goodbye, Barry

What 'tis to wave Goodbye and not to know
That but a part returns, while onward goes
A soul once held by this; what 'tis to go
And gaze upon the face that 'mid the throes
Of tearing and of hurt for aye was dimmed
In but a cosmic second that some hand
Let tap upon the clock, that Hist'ry trimmed
In this its heavy clipping: 'tis to stand
Alone upon the shore of this wide world
With more than half e'er lost; 'tis to be tossed
To Facts of dismal glaring, and be hurled
Across a morrow's barrier that, uncrossed,
Had left all time in peace – 'tis, friend, to cease
To be again, for Pain knows no release.

19/10

There are tears in things

(for Ellen)

When on and on I think as on the whole
The heart of man and woman knows not well
Its might to wield aright; when soul and soul
Together work on heav'n not much, but hell
Of such as only wedded bosoms know;
When I behold a holding not wherein
Fond heart on heart can rest, wherein can flow
A meaning and high Song with ne'er a din,
But well perfected Pain, again, again
Upon the damnèd air where fiend and friend
All, all commingled play: then this my pain
Of knowing what few know seems ne'er to end.
For, sister, we know more of this strange art
Of holding soul to soul though so apart.

25/10

Σιώπα, πεφίμωσο

(Silent, be still, Mk 4, 39)

There are too many words upon the earth,
And in the air much noise that need not be
The all of all that is, for less is worth
A little more than more that would not see
When better 'tis to end, and we, made still,
Hear oft a depth ill echoed when high din
'Neath morphine strong makes dull the raging ill
That we avoid in Void that gapes within.
We are not well when held in volume loud
That hears naught but its voice, and we do more
In leaving much undone, for oft the crowd
Of thoughts that walked the mind a lighter store
Of Meaning bore than but a little thing
Heard well, heard very well, and left to cling.

26/10

The vigil of a vigil

When I recall the night that I did wait
Upon a moment heavy that would come
To pierce the æons long, to seal the fate
Of small anointed hands 'neath Hist'ry's dome,
And when I look upon the moments trapped
Since that fair hour, the pow'r, the sound, the
heat,
The tingling in the air that there was trapped
In soft a mitred touch where much did meet,
Then as I tuck this burse and Chalice veil
To sleep till morrow's rays, wherein again
An ancient mischief will o'er Haste prevail
And bid pause long where yet a Lamb is slain,
I see a Hand upon a well-known land
Called Providence, wherein our blunders stand.

30/10

Singed

(by rays felt during *Missa cantata* at Bd Columba's altar)

What is a place, a spot upon the globe
That onward turns and pauses for no man?
What is it yet to wear an ancient robe
And stand upon a step that stepping can
From buried time yet hear? What is a stone
Hewn well to hold high force, hid workings strange?
What is, I say, a place to stand alone
Upon a land once known, 'neath th'old ray's range?
'Tis to be on a moving æon still,
Unshoved by Hurry's haste; 'tis to lean on
A second as it comes; 'tis to let thrill
Old tingles that once passed, for here's redone
A work that once worked well and works again
With ancient mastery we thought too plain.

9/11

Shaken to our foundations

(during Mass)

To start upon a journey and arrive
Upon another shore, where evermore
No journeying will be; to be alive
In but a severed part, to knock the door
Not of this place of prayer but of a shrine
Beyond our gazing's pow'r, where hours shall roll
In sep'rate way aye on; no more to shine
A ray of goodness here, but there to stroll
Upon the beams that made us: this, my friend,
Is, was, thy sudden lot; this was the all
Of one more beat that, coming not, the end
Of breathing e'ermore sealed, and thee did call
Across a cloud or two that hides a face
That in a twinkle eyed a wide, wide space.

29/11

Each has his tale

I have heard many meanings in the air,
But meanings of my own bade them not be.
There oft were o'er my ears yet moving there
High syllables of Sense sent unto me
But bid not enter in – therein there lay
A noise of answering that high did ring
E'en while each new word came, and kept at bay
Was aught that unto sound was found to cling.
And thus it is that knowing all before
New knowledge might have come, I now know all
ever knew, and know today no more
Than yesterday when yesterday did call
For but an hour to be, to be but heard,
For knowledge knew not all, that missed a word.

24/11

Their own tongue has brought them to ruin

(Infirmavit eos lingua eorum, Ps 63[64], 9)

There are too many noises upon earth,
And fewer more would hold, for more can say
A sound well found rebounding in full worth
Of being wanted, waited, than said aye
The tongue that rested never. We say all
But only when in poise, for noise falls well
When aimed and held and deftly left to fall
Upon a pause precise, that did not yell.
For talk is of two silences oft made,
And I heard more in gazing on an eye
And waiting for an uttering well weighed
Than e'er was heard when sound was running high.
For soul embraces soul upon a pause,
While noise was but of yawned annoyance cause.

10/1/9

Fy Annwyl Alun

Beth ydyw gair ar ddalen, a hen sain
A glywyd gynt yng ngwynt hen barthau mwyn?
Beth ydyw sill ar lythyr, ac ôl main
Ond croes neu ddwy mewn cusan? Beth yw swyn
Ysgrifen hoff ar amlen lle bu oes
Yn aros gynt am arall oes i ddod
A bod am byth yn leddfiad hiraedd loes
Dymuniad a dymuniad allai fod?
A beth yw hyn, fwyn angel, yn y gair
'Chwanegwyd mewn un sill mor fer a hir?
Ai piau chwaer ei brawd a brawd ei chwaer
Ym mhellter cell a phurdeb dyddiau hir
Un angel na cha'dd sylw, na cha'dd wledd
Ymorffwys yn hir wên cyfarwydd wedd?

10/1

Mischief at Mellifont

(with Dom Amedeo, O. Cist.)

These stones have heard before these melodies,
And silence ever old yet echoes well
The chant of brethren young, for stones like these
Were not meant thus to lie, for very Hell
Alone knew these to silence, where for long
They these same chants once echoed, vibrant each
With tremors of great age, the sages' song
That bright illumined copies sight did teach.
And brother that helps brother in high sin
Of strange derangèd magic lately banned
For that howled sounds electric and sweet din
It suited not, shall, suited, placid, stand
In colour known, in mischief known, alone
And not alone upon nought but a stone.

18/1

I am a king, where is my honour?

There are too many meddlings in this land
Of otherness, where bother is no more,
For that 'tis not henceforth to stand
On sacred ground, where what was thought before
To be all else by some was found today
A part, a part all plain and rude
Of workaday befriending, ending, nay
In haste, where waste is all that is not lewd.
O! glory of a Godhead now made man
At last, and blasted well from His high throne
Too distant for our time! Ah! blessèd ban
On all that is not known and is no show...
We have tamed the Beyond, and with a wand
Bid God be cool, and like a fool here stand.

21/1

Edrych dros y môr

(wrth fynd i'r cwfaint)

Mor agos ac mor bell, yr Henwlad fwyn,
Na clywir mwy ei sain ond yn y cof
A geidw ddoe ac echdoe fydd yn dwyn
Yfory'n ôl i'w plith... Pa bryd y dof
Nid yn y cof ond yn y cnawd yn ôl
I gôl hen leisiau cu, hen erwau fu
Yn rhan rhyw fodd ohonom? Hynod ffôl
Ias oriau glas ieuenctid gorffwyll hy' –
A bennodd ymhen eiliad oes i ddod
Heb ddod yn ôl i'r unig dyner fan
Lle dylai fod, ac er hir grwydro rhod
Gwareiddiad a dysg Dyn, wrth droedio glan
Yr Ynys Werdd, mi glywaf gerd hen dir
A llais hen heresi sy'n rhyfedd wir.

28/1
(gŵyl San Tomos Acwin)

Te lo prometto

What is a promise, what a word once heard
Or read upon an instrument so small
And mighty in its call? What stray beat stirred
My thumb to send a pledge beyond recall
Across the waves and clouds that sever well
Two medics' worlds? What hurled a yearn so far
Into a breast well known, that it might tell
Its tale of ne'er being shown where yearnings are?
Nay, nay, I yearn not, sister, thee to touch
Or watch or fondle where much heat may be,
But I'd thee kindle with a fondle such
As is not made of matter eye may see.
For I have promised, and this word shall keep,
To sing a big big child again to sleep.

4/2

Be still

There are but words upon the empty air,
And engines mute, in cuteness of small frame,
A din and babble tap while trapping e'er
The currents of stray thought. The cell became
The agora of earth where mirth was sought
In wit well chiselled, sent far o'er the skies
To pull a smile a little while from nought
But detonated thought bid blast sad eyes.
Yet though there be a healing in a spark
Of madness sent to jerk, and fondling keen
In little strokes of loving in a mark
I will not foul the virgin sound of Dark,
For night was made for seeing, and much light
Is glare too high, too nigh, where sound is sight.

5/2

I was silent, not opening my lips

(Obmutui et non aperiam os meum, quoniam tu fecisti,

Ps 38[39], 9)

To let it be is to be utterly
A being bid to be and wholly be,
And joy that came in laughing merrily
Ne'er high was oft as what came soft to me
In but a gaze of knowing: there is more
In keeping still, in keeping stillness heard,
In hearing th'uttered thought sealed 'neath the door
Of heeded Mind that needed not the word,
Than in a howlèd Distance – nay, to cling
And grasp and clasp all loudly is to hold
Afar the all that comes, and more did bring
A rest well held than rousèd darings bold.
And I will lay my head upon a pause,
And aye oppose no more a gentle cause.

7/2

Et sunt quorum non est memoria

(- perierunt quasi non fuerint, Sirach 44, 9)

To pass this way and leave upon a day
No blob or mark upon the map of age;
To be and to have been, and to be aye
A having been that on the ling'ring page
Of colour and of ink left not a trace;
To be no more a sound from 'yond the grave
That rocks a slumber long; to be a face
That will not beam from rays some lens did save –
To be, I say, no more, and no more be
Here wanted upon earth: 'twere this the all
Of haste in wasted being, for I see
That we were not here meant to be so small
As not to be twice seen, for having been
Need not be th'all writ e'er on Chronos' screen.

12/2

An rud a líonas an tsuíl líonann sé an croí

(What fills the eye fills the heart)

What is a face, a little little space
Upon the cosmos wide, where hides the all
Of what, beheld again, held healing grace
Of God and man commingled; what the call
Of cord and vocal cord that tingled deep
In th'echoing abyss; what is a kiss
But soul that touched a soul; what is't to weep
But molten soul to ooze in mangled bliss?
And what are eyes but windows ne'er forgot
In which I see th'unseen, in which I know
That I am known on earth, for mirth comes not
So often in a blast and in a glow
As in a rest of little little rays
That warmed the planet all in smallest ways?

14/2
(meditating on 1Th 3, 10)

The matter

There is a secret in the universe
That few, 'twould seem, have known; there is a way
To be and not to be that would reverse
The accidents of being, ever aye,
Were th'accidental called but by its name
And not the essence thought; there is a pow'r
Within the mind to send back whence it came
The misery that held a heavy hour:
And 'tis but this, and 'tis a bliss to own,
For that the damnèd moments it did spare –
'Tis this, I say, the leaving yet unblown
The all that might ignite; it is to dare
Not much to mind when matter of great weight
Was seen to weigh p'haps less than matters great.

17/2

A little lap

*(Bangor is a place of memories. I sometimes marvel as I look back—
how many parallel, virtual futures it once contained.)*

Will I yet see a place I knew so well
And in it once again a little face
Unchanged by all the years, that could all tell
From looking at my own? Will I embrace
A little world I knew, whereon an hour
I rested in a dream, within a heat
Not of a passion made but of a pow'r
That somehow I well knew: will little feet
Walk gently this old way and bring again
What was not felt on earth since we moved on
From these strange moments huge in joy and pain
For that they came but once, and left undone
The morrow that they held, the sorrow held
At bay awhile, while I a smile beheld?

21/2

תהום־אל־תהום קורא

(Abyssus abyssum invocat)

There is a call upon the darkest night,
A cry unheard that from the earth ascends;
There is in silence long a knowing quite
That day did never grasp; the dark a heeding lends
To many things unheard, and I know all
When all, all, all alone, when shown full blown
Is vision bright, is sight known by no ball
Or retina in gaze where haze is known.
For in the night where light blinds not the eye
The colour of the mind is bright and fair,
And fairer still when travel needs no sky
Or moving hence where dense is sense aglare.
For I behold in holding in holding nought on earth
That chasms were not heard by roarèd mirth.

22/2

Y gorau o athrawon

(Dewi Pŵel)

Y mae mewn wyneb hoff hen ddyddiau fu
Yn gwawrio gynt ar fore oes, na ddaw
Ond unwaith yn ein dydd, ac oriau cu
Ni ddônt yn ôl ond yn y cof na thaw
Ei furmur maith hyd fachlud hyn o ddydd
A ddaw am dro drwy'r rhod: atgofion Bod,
Cysgodion haul a fu – ond hyn a fydd
Yfory ac yfory eto'n dod.
Ac eto weithiau Ddoe nid ffoi yn llwyr
O olwg Heddiw wna, ac yn hen wedd
A ddeil, a ddeil ynghýnn yn oriau'r hwyr
Daw atsain emyn dôn am ryfedd hedd
Lle'r unir tad a mab tu draw i'r llen
Lle na fydd dadlau 'nghylch anthemau'r nen.

2/3

A presto

Come, little one, and rest awhile a soul
Much wounded by much pain – again come home
To simple things, where clings unchanged and whole
The all of Yesterday: come, stay and roam
No more upon the passions of an hour
Or two of hurting joy, for cloy shall all
That was not made for thee, and there is pow'r
Again in pleasures little, simple, small,
And angels shall yet grin and giggle well
To heart at heart of night a merry song
Not made of metal marred by scarrèd Hell
But of a virgin lullaby heard long
Long, long ago where thou wast meant to be,
For angels know their home, and roam not free.

6/3

Life is far too important
to be taken seriously

When once upon an æon Wisdom thought
Upon a hominid that could but be
If from a drowsèd dream an utter nought
Were uttered into being, did He see
Within the twinkle of His ancient eye
A corner of a cosmos where the blast
Of damnèd rayons could be let pass by
Without being th'all of all unto the last?
And did to placid might a sparkle bright
Of naughtiness in the Trisagion
Come in a dark stark moment, to ignite
E'en seraphs in their play, and to egg on
The dwellers of a strange derangèd isle
That while the cosmos cracked lay back awhile?

10/3

Heresy

Let none on earth e'er say that grace is dead
In pulpits high of lowest of low Church
Or that the sound of utterance well said
Had not the pow'r of sacrament to search to search
The marrows of a soul – let none, I say,
With sharpened nib the cords umbilical
Of new-born babes light sever, for a day
Whereon a soul is born, reborn from Hell calls all.
And though it be well said that water laves
And fullness of high touch the clutch of God
Doth hold the all in poise, a noise that saves
Upon a day the years and years that plod
T'ward nether graceless land the Saviour's hand
Did bless, thrice bless and through blest Schism command.

13/3

Gloria

(Gloria Polo's return from the dead)

I hold within my hand a mighty thing
That should not be, that has no right to be,
That men would not have be, to which doth cling
A powder of high sulphur none can see
But only thinly smell, for Hell in rage
Is passing howling by, and I behold
Upon a page a cry that shall not age
As men's dim sound so frenzied and so old.
For here no ageing comes, but ever young
The morrow long that waits, and gates not seen
Reveal 'hind seals most huge the very song
That doth but dawn upon dawns having been.
For there is long cacophony where day was bright,
And song most hugely wrong closed oft the night.

16/3
(Testimony found at www.gloriapolo.com)

The problem

(La crisi di fede è tutt'una con la mancanza di vita interiore. Senza vita interiore non vi è capacità di agire. Mancanza di vita interiore è mancanza di vita di Grazia: chi non vive, nulla può fare...)

There was a word once heard deep in a soul,
A word that came from 'yond the skies, a word
To calm all words, wherein at last the whole
Of all e'er said or thought was strangely heard.
And, kneeling in the night where unchanged years
Pass yet unhurried on, I hear it come
Again in ancient pow'r, for many tears
In vain were lost in lands far far from home.
For I perceive that had this little sound
Been heard by many souls that hovered by
Upon the rim of being, peace ne'er found
Could 'neath the bounds of thinking have stood nigh.
For all is here upon a truth, the all
Of truth, the all. For all big words were small.

17/3

La crisi...: Words heard by the saintly friend of Paul VI, Mons. Ottavio Michelini, in 1976: "Crisis in faith is one and the same with lack of interior life. Without interior life there is no capacity to act. Lack of interior life is lack of a life of Grace: he who does not live can do nothing."

Μυστήριον

I have perceived the all upon a day
Wherein there was a pause, a time to be
Hard by a sound that did not die away
As quickly as it came, for now I see
Where song too long was blind, and I behold
Upon the blobs of music deeper things
Than what a vibrant cord alone can hold,
For unto thought not wrought more thinking clings.
And God fled oft where softer noise came not
To stroke the Master's feelings, there where much
Felt depth of chasmèd meaning was forgot
In pressing on a stress of beauty such
That beauty 'twas no more, but only stench
That calmèd souls in prayer from prayer did wrench.

22/3
(after imperfect chant at high Mass)